Hardwick Hall

Derbyshire

THE NATIONAL TRUST

More glass than wall

Pride in place

As you climb the hill towards Hardwick, the first things you see are the tops of the towers bearing the silhouetted initials ES for Elizabeth, Countess of Shrewsbury, better known as Bess of Hardwick.

Bess of Hardwick and the house she built are inseparable. She was born at the Old Hall in about 1527, and it was here as a formidable widow in her sixties that she returned, after four judicious marriages had equipped her with the wealth to build a new house next to the Old Hall. Hardwick New Hall is her proud memorial, celebrating in stone her rise from an obscure gentry family to the rank and riches of a countess. Its decoration proclaimed her loyalty to her namesake, Queen Elizabeth, and it was also intended to support a dynasty founded by her favourite son, Sir William Cavendish.

A perfect prodigy

Hardwick Hall is perhaps the most perfect of all the Elizabethan 'prodigy houses'. To design it, Bess chose the greatly gifted Robert Smythson, a mason by training but one of the first Englishmen to be described as 'architect'; and she poured a lifetime of her own experience of building into the project. The exterior is relatively plain; what makes Hardwick unforgettable are its height and symmetry, the ever-changing silhouette of its six towers, and the huge expanses of window glass that glitter magically on a sunny evening and inspired the famous rhyme, 'Hardwick Hall, more glass than wall'.

A house of treasures

Uniquely among Elizabethan houses, Hardwick retains the textures of its original decoration – huge Flemish tapestries, Persian table-carpets, painted wall-hangings, coloured plaster friezes, inlaid furniture, rows of original portraits, and the finest collection of 16th- and early 17th-century needlework in the world. Many can still be identified in the detailed inventory that Bess had compiled in 1601.

The Devonshire inheritance

On Bess's death in 1608, Hardwick passed into the Cavendish family, who were created Earls, and then Dukes, of Devonshire. They chose Chatsworth as their principal home, but

(Right) Bess of Hardwick in old age. She is wearing the 'fore ropes of greate perle' listed among her jewellery in 1593

(Above) Hardwick Hall from the south-west

continued to cherish Hardwick. When they came to rebuild Chatsworth from the late 17th century, they transferred many of its Elizabethan furnishings to Bess's house. Hardwick remained an unmodernised 16th-century showpiece which attracted legends, most famously that Mary, Queen of Scots had stayed here during her captivity (although she had in fact been executed before the house was built).

In 1811 the Bachelor 6th Duke inherited nine large houses, but he had a special affection for Hardwick, perhaps because it had been a favourite refuge of his mother, the unhappy Duchess Georgiana. Much of what you now see at Hardwick is the result of his efforts to enhance and preserve the Elizabethan romance of Bess's house. Many of his changes, like setting up the canopy in the Long Gallery, were unhistorical, but they are effective nevertheless, and have now become part of the history of the place. He expressed his pride and affection in his own highly entertaining *Handbook*.

Conservation in action

The Bachelor Duke began the campaign of textile conservation which was taken up most devotedly in the early 20th century by the last member of the family to live here, Duchess Evelyn. When the National Trust acquired Hardwick from the 11th Duke via the Treasury in 1959, it inherited the Cavendish family's responsibility for preserving not just the fabric and contents of the house, but also its potent, but fragile atmosphere.

Visiting Hardwick

With its high ceilings and draughty windows, Hardwick is undeniably a cold house, more enjoyable to visit than to live in. Visitors have been welcomed from the start. Their reactions have varied: the 18th-century taste-maker Horace Walpole saw only 'vast rooms, no taste'; most, however, agree with a more recent critic, Anthony Wells-Cole, who concluded that 'for sheer excitement there is no Elizabethan house in England to rival Hardwick'.

High Great Chamber
The grandest reception room, where Bess greeted and entertained guests. The decoration makes flattering references to the Queen, whom Bess hoped would honour it with her presence.

Banqueting Room
A rooftop chamber in which Bess and her most honoured dinner guests could enjoy a final 'banquet' course of sweetmeats.

Second floor: *state rooms*
(windows four panes high)
The sequence of rooms on this floor copies that of a royal palace: public presence chamber, more restricted private chamber and, finally, bed-chamber (for intimates only), with adjoining closets. The decoration features classical history and myth and symbolic representations of the virtues Bess prized, particularly Patience and Charity.

First floor: *family rooms*
(three panes high)
Contains Bess's bedroom (not shown) and private dining room. Decoration primarily illustrates Biblical themes.

Ground floor: *servants' quarters* (two panes high)
Originally, the most prominent feature was the heraldic overmantel in the Hall linking the Hardwick and Cavendish families. Otherwise, these service rooms were sparsely decorated.

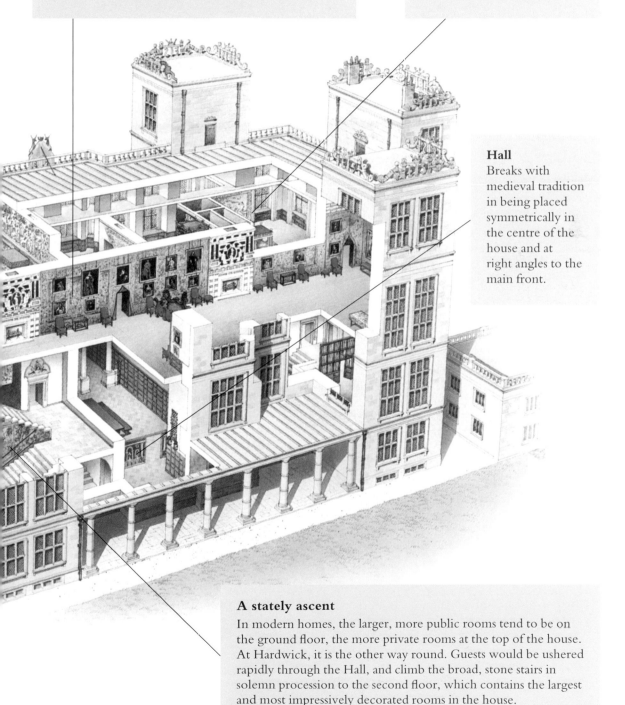

Long Gallery
A place to exercise in bad weather, enjoy the view and the royal and family portraits hung here. The present arrangement of the pictures was largely the work of the Bachelor Duke in the early 19th century.

Blue Room
Bess's principal state bedroom, known in her time as the Pearl Bedchamber from its pearl-embroidered bed.

Hall
Breaks with medieval tradition in being placed symmetrically in the centre of the house and at right angles to the main front.

A stately ascent
In modern homes, the larger, more public rooms tend to be on the ground floor, the more private rooms at the top of the house. At Hardwick, it is the other way round. Guests would be ushered rapidly through the Hall, and climb the broad, stone stairs in solemn procession to the second floor, which contains the largest and most impressively decorated rooms in the house.

Tour of the house

The Hall

The Hall was used in Elizabethan days as both servants' hall and entrance hall. The wooden tables and forms relate to the former; the stone screen and fireplace were intended to give dignity to the latter.

The *stone screen* was carved by William Griffin in 1597 and is a remarkably pure piece of classical design for its date. It supports a gallery connecting the Drawing Room to the Dining Room (Low Great Chamber).

Furniture

One Elizabethan *table and two forms* are still in the Hall, but the massive oak *central table*, its top made of only two pieces of wood each 8.4 metres long, is mid-17th-century.

The 17th-century carved *wooden chairs* are all 19th-century introductions. Among them is the *'Revolution' chair* brought from the Cock and Pynot Inn at Whittington, near Chesterfield, and said (dubiously) to have been the chair in which the 4th Earl of Devonshire sat when plotting to bring William of Orange over as King of England in 1688.

The great iron-bound wooden *chest* by the entrance was probably used for storing money.

Armour

The armour is a miscellaneous selection mainly of the 17th century, brought down from one of the turrets in the 19th century. Between the windows at the east end of the Hall are the accoutrements of Lord John Cavendish, the 9th Duke's brother, who was killed in the First World War.

Pictures

Opposite the fireplace hangs a portrait of *Bess of Hardwick*, probably painted about 1580, a decade before she built the house.

1601 The Hall

The room was hung with tapestries of 'personages with forestwork' (possibly the 15th-century Hunting Tapestries now in the Victoria & Albert Museum). The furniture consisted of three long tables, six forms, four wall sconces, two chandeliers and two firedogs.

Prominent over the chimneypiece is a plasterwork *overmantel* of the Hardwick coat of arms, surmounted by a countess's coronet and supported by two stags with real antlers. A stag with a collar of wild roses, or eglantines, was the Hardwick family crest; three eglantines also form the upper half of the Hardwick coat of arms, and the flowers occur frequently in decoration and embroidery around the house. (The white, five-petalled eglantine, a symbol of chastity, was adopted by Queen Elizabeth as one of her emblems, and this may have provided Bess with an added incentive for its use.) The Hardwick stags were later adopted by the Cavendishes as supporters.

Embroideries

The *wooden screens* at the far end of the Hall contain pieces from two sets of hangings originally made for Chatsworth in the 1570s. They are made out of a patchwork of pieces of velvet, cloth of gold and figured silk, partly cut out of medieval copes. They are the most important Elizabethan embroideries in the house, and among the most important in existence.

On the side facing the main body of the Hall are *two hangings* showing famous and worthy heroines between figures personifying their virtues – a theme that must have been congenial to Bess. To the left is Penelope with Perseverance and Patience, to the right Lucretia with Chastity and Liberality.

On the other side of the screens are *panels of figures of virtues* contrasted with historic characters who were thought to embody their contrary vices. Faith has her contrary, Mahomet, prostrate at her feet, and

Temperance has the effeminate Sardanapalus in a similar position. Inset panels show *Mahomet walking with his disciples* and *Sardanapalus feasting while his palace burns*.

Framed on the wall opposite the fireplace are *two panels* embroidered in cross-stitch, showing the *Judgement of Solomon* and the *Sacrifice of Isaac*. They are in the style of a professional workshop, probably French: Solomon is watched by courtiers dressed in the style of the French court of Henri III.

On the fireplace wall are *framed embroideries*; the panel to the right of the fireplace shows the story of the Prodigal Son, but the other has not been identified. They were probably made as carpets to drape over cupboards.

Tapestries

The present hangings consist of a set of *Scenes of Country Life*, from the workshop of Jakob Geubels I, and *Proverbs*. Both sets are from cartoons by Jacob Jordaens. They were brought from Chatsworth by the 6th Duke.

(Right) Penelope is one of five immensely rare appliqué hangings, which Bess displayed in the Withdrawing Chamber upstairs. She identified strongly with this patient heroine of classical mythology

The threads of time
The Hardwick needlework

View now or at the end of your tour.

The ground-floor rooms to the south of the Hall are devoted to exhibitions describing the history of Hardwick and displaying part of the house's unique collection of 16th- and early 17th-century embroideries. Most were executed about 1570–1640; the earlier ones in this period were made for Chatsworth and brought over by Bess in the 1590s to furnish her new house at Hardwick; the later ones date from the time of Christian, Countess of Devonshire, the wife of Bess's grandson, the 2nd Earl. Originally, they served many purposes, especially as wall- or bed-hangings, table-carpets and cushion covers.

Who made them?

Bess probably always had one or more full-time embroiderers on her staff. In 1598 'Webb the imbroderer' was paid 18s 4d a quarter, a wage which put him lower on the scale than the porter, butler or blacksmith and higher than the laundress and glazier. An entry

(Above) This strapwork panel is decorated in cloths of gold and silver with Bess's monogram and eglantine rose symbol

(Below) The needlework cushion listed in the 1601 inventory as the 'Fancie of a Fowler'. Like much of the decoration at Hardwick, it is based on a continental engraving (not on show)

in the accounts for 1591 shows that an embroiderer had a chamber and inner chamber allotted to him in the Old Hall. Many of the smaller embroideries were probably the work of Bess herself and her gentlewomen, perhaps with the aid of a professional to set out the design. In spite of widespread belief to the contrary, there is nothing that can be positively attributed to Mary, Queen of Scots, except for two panels which may only have come to Hardwick in the 19th century.

How were they made?

A number of different techniques were used. The most impressive of these is the use of applied work, especially in the form of velvets and patterned silks cut out and made into pictorial wall-hangings. The velvets and silks used are mostly Italian 15th- and 16th-century weavings, and some certainly came from church vestments; in 1557 Bess's second husband, Sir William Cavendish, bought copes originating from the dissolved religious house at Lilleshall in Shropshire, and more vestments came through her third husband, Sir William St Loe, in the 1560s. Only the woven silks and velvets were cut up; the embroidered 'orphreys' (ornamental borders) and hoods were put aside and still survive at Hardwick, made up into panels described in the 1601 inventory and elsewhere as 'church work'.

The inventory refers to 'nyne payres of beames for imbroiderers' in the wardrobe on the second floor of the New Hall. On these frames must have been worked in cross-stitch many of the cushion covers at Hardwick. Another very common product of the Hardwick embroiderers were panels of red velvet on which strips of cloth of silver were sewn down to form interlacing quatrefoils and rectangles, edged with gilt cord and filled in with flowers and leaves.

A much less common technique was to set out strapwork and interlacing patterns on plain velvet, outline them with couched embroidery in silk or velvet, and then paint the velvet in contrasting colours.

Fragments of medieval church vestments (not on show)

The embroideries are profusely decorated with Bess's and other monograms, and the arms, crests and supporters of Hardwick, Cavendish and Talbot, especially the Hardwick stag and eglantine. Motifs were often derived from continental engravings.

The Evidence Room

A small room used to examine the documents housed in the adjacent Muniment Room.

The Muniment Room

From 1603 this room housed the 'muniments' (title deeds and other documents) for the Hardwick estates. They were filed in the built-in drawers, which were probably installed in the mid-17th century.

The Tobit Room

This room contains the magnificent Tobit table-carpet. The carpet, which tells the story of Tobias (see p. 27), was made in 1579 for Bess, while she was living with her fourth husband, the Earl of Shrewsbury, at Sheffield Manor.

The Duke's Room

The room is named after the 9th Duke, who stayed at Hardwick every autumn for the shooting. A man who liked peace and quiet, he found it in this remote little sitting room. The room contains a display of the later history of Hardwick and the Ivan Turner Miniature Furniture Collection.

The Main Staircase

Tapestries

The set along the first flight of steps shows the story of **Hero and Leander**. The scenes depicted include the first meeting of the two lovers, who lived on either side of the Hellespont; Leander swimming across on his nightly assignation with Hero; and Hero's discovery of Leander's drowned body. They were made at the factory founded by James I at Mortlake, Surrey, from a design of the 1620s by Francis Cleyn, which remained popular until well after 1660. The Hardwick set is one of the later examples and was brought here by the 6th Duke from Chatsworth.

Prominent on the Drawing Room landing are two splendid late 17th-century tapestries,

Bess and her honoured guests would have climbed these broad stairs in stately procession to reach the High Great Chamber

possibly of Brussels manufacture, showing two unidentified scenes from Roman history.

Running up from the Drawing Room landing are four panels of *Hatton Garden tapestry* showing children at play. One piece is marked 'hatton garden' and signed with the initials of Francis Poyntz; the tapestries must date from between 1679 and 1685, when Poyntz and the Great Wardrobe, of which he was in charge, were in Hatton Garden. Opposite them, across the Staircase, a thin strip showing a portion of a lion hunt is all that survives of what must have been an early 16th-century Flemish tapestry of the highest quality; it would originally have formed part of a set depicting the story of Vasco da Gama or the Portuguese in India, which records show was very popular, and have been woven at Tournai.

On the big intermediate landing is a selection of *Flemish verdure tapestries* of the mid-16th century; the one with a landscape along the top had been cut into strips and used to fill gaps in the Gallery.

To the right of the entrance to the High Great Chamber, and above the Staircase, is a *Flemish, probably Brussels, tapestry* of the second half of the 16th century, showing sheep-shearing.

Above the door is a *Flemish Gothic panel* of the first quarter of the 16th century showing, in strip-cartoon fashion, David having his son

The tapestries on the upper flight of stairs were made at Hatton Garden in London in 1679–85

Solomon crowned king, and Solomon, after his father's death, ordering the building of the Temple of Jerusalem. This and the lion-hunt fragment are the earliest tapestries at Hardwick.

Table-carpet

On the intermediate landing is a long table covered with a Turkish Star Ushak carpet, probably of the 16th century. This is one of three Turkish carpets at Hardwick which may be survivors of the 32 'Turkey carpets' mentioned in the 1601 inventory. Most of these were used, as the Ushak is today, to cover tables or cupboards.

Metalwork

The immensely elaborate *late medieval lock* is probably German, and it remains uncertain whether it was on the door to the High Great Chamber from the start or is a later addition.

1601

There were originally no tapestries hanging on the Staircase. There was also little here in the way of furniture or fittings, except beds, forms and tables on the landings, for waiting or sleeping servants; the beds were made 'to turn up like Chestes' in order to conceal them during the day. The stairs were lit by a 'great glass Lanthorne', but the present one is a modern copy of the original lantern on the Chapel landing.

The High Great Chamber

This is the most undilutedly Elizabethan room in Hardwick, and the most magnificent. The first thing that strikes one on entering it is its enormous size. A roomy five-bedroomed house could comfortably be fitted into it. The other rooms on this floor are in the same vein of lavishness. They are royal in their conception. The accepted accommodation of an English royal palace consisted of six rooms, a presence chamber for state, a privy chamber where the monarch normally ate, and received more favoured visitors, a withdrawing chamber, a bedchamber and a gallery. Unlike most Elizabethan houses, Hardwick could have provided the whole suite on a splendid scale, with the High Great Chamber acting as Presence Chamber, and the adjoining With-drawing Chamber (the ceiling of which originally rose as high as that of the High Great Chamber, as 'Privy Chamber').

The grandest and biggest house in England was Theobalds in Hertfordshire, long since demolished, the home of Elizabeth's Lord Treasurer and trusted counsellor, Lord

1601 *The High Great Chamber*

Bess and her guests ate off a 'long table of white wood' covered with two carpets (probably alternatives), 'a fayre turkie Carpet' and a 'fayre long Carpet of silk nedlework with gold frenge, lyned with Crimson taffetie sarcenet'. When the table was in use, the carpets would have been covered or replaced by the diaper or damask tablecloths mentioned in the inventory. Bess sat in a 'chare of nedlework with gold and silk frenge' complete with footstool, and for the rest of the company there were six forms and sixteen stools, elaborately upholstered and cushioned. The only other furniture in the room was a looking glass (a rarity in Elizabethan days) decorated with the royal arms, an 'inlayde table in the window', a 'Cubberd guilt and carved with tills' and 'a payre of brass Andyrons' or firedogs, which can almost certainly be identified with the present magnificent brass ones, drawn in the room by Grimm in 1785. The 'Cubberd guilt' is probably the Du Cerceau cupboard, now in the Withdrawing Chamber.

Palace for an uncrowned queen?

What was Bess aiming at? A possible explanation lies in her little granddaughter Arbella Stuart, by right of her father a royal Stuart, with a claim to succession to the English throne which some thought better (because she had been born in England) than that of her cousin James. Elizabeth splendidly received and fêted at Hardwick, Arbella declared her heir, further royal visits and the subsequent glorification of the Cavendish family – something like this may lie behind the great echoing rooms at Hardwick, waiting, as it turned out, for a Queen who never came, and a royal succession which never materialised.

Burghley. Elizabeth stayed there constantly, and treated it, in effect, as an alternative royal palace. In 1587 Bess's son Sir Charles Cavendish sent his mother the measurements of the Great Chamber at Theobalds, and Bess built the High Great Chamber in the Old Hall to approximately the same size. But her High Great Chamber in the New Hall was far larger – even though Hardwick was a much smaller house.

The *decoration* was not completed until 1599, two years after Bess had moved into the house. The room was designed as a unity, with frieze, tapestry and chimneypiece fitted together into a whole glowing with incident and rich colour; the colours have faded, and the contrast between the sophistication of the tapestry and the crude but evocative realism of the frieze is less strong than it must once have been.

Frieze: *loyalty in plaster*

Its theme is the forest, with the court of Diana prominent on the north side (above the canopy) amid attendant deer, lions, elephants, camels and other animals, and elsewhere scenes of deer- and boar-hunting, and of country life. The court of Diana, the virgin goddess and huntress, is probably a deliberate allusion to Elizabeth, the Virgin Queen.

To either side of the window recess, and rather more skilfully modelled than the rest of the frieze, are allegorical figures of Venus chastising Cupid, and Summer, based on Flemish engravings by Crispin van der Passe

from designs by Martin de Vos. The hunting scenes elsewhere in the frieze are based on engravings by Philip Galle after Johannes Stradanus.

The frieze was almost certainly modelled by Abraham Smith and his assistants and probably coloured by John Ballechouse, who was probably also responsible for the narrow strip of flat surface painting under the ceiling on the south and west sides. The original paint survives, much faded except for a small area in the south-east corner which has been clumsily restored and waxed.

Chimneypiece

The overmantel displays the royal arms supported by a lion and a dragon. The relatively simple chimneypiece below was probably carved by Thomas Accres.

Tapestries

The tapestries have hung in the High Great Chamber since 1601 and may be a set bought by Bess from Sir William Pickering before 1572. They are Brussels tapestries of the second half of the 16th century, from designs in the style of Michael Coxce. They have the Brussels mark and various weavers' marks, unidentifiable except for one mark of Nicholas Hellinck. They depict the story of Ulysses.

Ulysses taking leave of his wife Penelope; no. 3 in the series of late 16th-century Brussels tapestries

ANTI-CLOCKWISE FROM ENTRANCE DOOR
(NUMBERS INDICATE NARRATIVE SEQUENCE):

1 *Ulysses kills a boar and is wounded in the leg*

2 *His attempt to escape the Trojan expedition by feigning madness and yoking a horse and ox together is exposed when he swerves the team to avoid his infant son*

4 *He identifies the young Achilles, whose mother has disguised him as a girl to save him from the Trojan expedition*

3 *He departs for Troy and takes leave of his wife and her parents*

6 *On his long and adventurous return from Troy he forces the enchantress Circe to restore his companions, whom she had turned into animals, to human form*

5 *At Troy he is awarded the armour of Achilles who has been killed in battle*

7 *He is shipwrecked, befriended by Princess Nausicaa, and given a new ship by her parents*

8 *After twenty years he is reunited with Penelope and his son, having killed the suitors who were trying to force her to remarry*

Hardwick matting

Hardwick gives its name to a type of rush-matting that was commonly used on the floors of grand rooms like the High Great Chamber in the late 16th and 17th centuries. Duchess Evelyn reintroduced the matting to Hardwick; it becomes brittle when dry, so requires regular watering.

Panelling

The panelling may have been introduced in the early 17th century in the time of the 1st Earl; the pilasters are additions, probably made by the 6th Duke. The panels are decorated with engravings consisting of a set of Roman emperors, and another of classical authors and philosophers.

Furniture

The *chairs and stools* are copies made in the 6th Duke's time (one is dated 1845) of originals

'For one winter I dine with my friends in this room, which was more dignified than entertaining, and, in spite of all precautions, exceeding cold.'

The 6th Duke

Eglantine table

Standing in the window bay, this is elaborately inlaid with musical instruments, sheets of music (one has the motet 'Oh Lord in Thee is all my trust' set for four parts), cards, chess and backgammon boards, an inkhorn, the arms of Talbot impaling Hardwick and Cavendish impaling Talbot, and the Cavendish, Hardwick and Talbot crests and mottoes. In the centre two Hardwick stags support the motto:

The redolent smele of Aeglantyne
We stagges exault to the deveyne

The table may have been made to commemorate the triple marriage of Bess to the Earl of Shrewsbury, Henry Cavendish to Grace Talbot, and Mary Cavendish to Gilbert Talbot in 1567. It may be the 'inlayde table' listed here in 1601 and has certainly been in the High Great Chamber since the 18th century.

arms of Countess Christian and her husband, the 2nd Earl. Such canopies had traditionally only been set up for royalty, or ambassadors, but in the 17th century dukes, marquesses and earls and their consorts began to affect them too. The Hardwick canopy was removed to Chatsworth, as 'too glaring' for the room, by the Bachelor Duke, brought back and restored as a bed canopy by Duchess Evelyn, but reinstated by the Trust in the High Great Chamber in the 1990s. Also in the room is the Countess's *state couch* with sadly worn embroidery and her arms painted amid simulated embroidery on the wooden ends. It was drawn by S. H. Grimm in 1785, when it was under a plainer canopy in the Long Gallery. The magnificent andirons were illustrated in their present position by Grimm at the same time, and are probably the 'payre of brass Andyrons' listed in 1601.

The two walnut *mirrors* hanging to either side of the window bay are late 17th-century English, as is the *longcase clock*, the works of which are dated 1697.

probably of the 17th century. The originals were fitted up in 1635, when an entry in Christian, Countess of Devonshire's account book records payment to 'George Savage the Imbroyderer' for seven weeks' work on the 'purple embroydered suite'. This embroidery was remounted for the 6th Duke on new brown velvet when the new chairs were made up; by then the original purple velvet had probably faded to brown.

The 6th Duke also remounted in similar fashion the great embroidered *canopy*, bearing the

(Right) Bess would have sat in state under a canopy like this, but it postdates her, having been made in the early 17th century for Christian Bruce, wife of the 2nd Earl. It was put up here by the Bachelor Duke in the 19th century after considerable modification

The Long Gallery

Measuring 51 metres long, 8 metres high and varying from 6.7 to 12 metres in width, the Hardwick Gallery is the largest (although not the longest) of surviving Elizabethan long galleries, and the only one to retain both its original tapestries and many of its original pictures.

The *frieze* above the chimneypiece and tapestries was probably painted by John Ballechouse in 1598. If the two splendid *chimneypieces*, with their delicate and beautiful alabaster statues of Justice and Mercy, are by Thomas Accres, they are the culmination of his work at Hardwick, but they are more probably by another carver and are the only internal features at Hardwick which are likely to have been designed by Robert Smythson. It is unlikely that the modelled plasterwork of the *ceiling* dates from Bess's time; it and similar ceilings at Hardwick may have been part of the undocumented alterations carried out by the 1st Earl after he inherited from Bess in 1608.

Tapestries

The thirteen tapestries showing the story of *Gideon and his triumph over the Midianites* were bought by Bess when in London in 1592 from Sir William Newport (later Hatton), the nephew and heir of Sir Christopher Hatton, Elizabeth's favourite and Lord Chancellor. Hatton had died in 1591 leaving an estate heavily encumbered with debts, and Bess bought at least three sets of tapestry from his heir: the Gideon set, the Abraham set now in the Green Velvet Room, and the 'personages' in

1601 The Gallery

It was sparsely furnished with two square inlaid tables, covered with carpets, three chairs, three low stools, a footstool, two forms, two mirrors, a little ivory table and a fire-screen. In each window was a window seat furnished with a richly embroidered cushion. The embroideries often took the form of pictures; a number of these survive.

the Drawing Room. The cost of the Gideon set was £326 15s 9d, from which £5 was deducted because Bess had to change the Hatton arms to her own. In fact all that was done was to cover the Hatton shields with pieces of cloth painted with Bess's arms, and to add painted horns and collars to the Hatton does to convert them into Hardwick stags.

The tapestries had been made for Hatton in 1578 and originally hung at Holdenby,

Northamptonshire, his principal house. They are 5.8 metres high, which is unusually large for tapestries, and are Flemish, probably made at Oudenarde. The colours have faded, and the story is almost impossible to make out because of the pictures that cover the tapestries.

At first they were probably unencumbered by pictures, but in the time of the 5th Duke the tapestries and all available wall space were covered with pictures of all dates.

'Stupendous and original'

The 6th Duke described how people on a tour of the house 'begin to get weary and to think they have done, and to want their luncheon; but they are awakened when the tapestry over the door at the North end of this room is lifted up, and they find themselves in this stupendous and original apartment.'

Pictures

The Long Gallery is perhaps the finest example in Britain of the traditional country-house picture gallery, hung in tiers with ancient portraits of the family and the famous. It looks unchanged since Bess's day, but in fact its present appearance was largely a romantic creation of the 5th and 6th Dukes in the early 19th century.

Bess's will mentions 37 portraits in the Long Gallery. So in her time the room was hung much more sparsely than we see it today – not over the tapestries, but probably on the window walls opposite. The portraits were mostly small, and more than half of them were of royalty. After Bess's death, her son William employed Rowland Lockey to paint over 30 pictures for Hardwick. Most were copies of family portraits, but they also included images of Mary, Queen of Scots and her relations, who assumed greater significance for the Cavendish family after the succession of Mary's son James to the English throne in 1603.

The first major influx of additional portraits took place under the 5th Duke. The 6th Duke went further, bringing together from his other various houses and from other parts of Hardwick pictures that would complement his historicising redecoration of the room. He hung them in tiers of two, three or more pictures, with little concern for visibility, because, as he wrote in his *Handbook*, 'The pictures, of little value separate, have become interesting as a series'.

Today, the older pictures comprise royal portraits that have been in the house since Bess's time. Foremost among them is the full-length of Queen Elizabeth (no. 35), probably from the workshop of Nicholas Hilliard, in one of the most extraordinary of her many extraordinary dresses; it was probably brought from London to Hardwick in 1599. There are also portraits of Bess's family and important relations. What purport to be images of 15th- and 16th-century Cavendishes turn out to be of historical figures such as Robert Dudley, Earl of Leicester, which were subsequently mislabelled to represent missing ancestors. The 5th and 6th Dukes added 17th-century portraits, which were thought

Thomas Hobbes, a philosopher servant

The philosopher and author of *Behemoth* and *Leviathan* entered the 2nd Earl's service when they were both young men just down from Oxford. According to John Aubrey, although ostensibly the Earl's tutor, Hobbes mainly 'rode a hunting and hawking with him and kept his privy purse ... His lord, who was a waster, sent him up and down to borrow money, and to get gentlemen to be bound for him, being ashamed to speak himself.' None the less the two men seem to have been genuinely fond of each other. After the 2nd Earl's premature death, Hobbes became tutor to his son, the 3rd Earl, who remained his patron and protector for the rest of his life. At the end of his long career he retired to Chatsworth and Hardwick. At Hardwick he used to sing prick-song very badly in his bed at night and to walk up and down the hill 'till he was in a great sweat, and then give the servants some money to rub him'. He believed these activities would preserve his life, and indeed he survived till the age of 91. When the family moved from Chatsworth to Hardwick during his last illness, he was carried on a feather bed into a coach, and moved with them. He died at Hardwick in 1679 and is buried in its parish church at Ault Hucknall, beneath an inscription which places his long service under two Earls of Devonshire before the fact that he was 'well known at home and abroad through the fame of his learning'. He is said to haunt the path under the walls of the Old Hall.

sufficiently historical to hang here. These are still primarily of dynastic interest, and the historical figures are aristocratic. The 6th Duke also placed here representatives of foreign ruling families.

The pictures include two portraits of Bess herself – painted as a pretty redhead in about 1560 (no. 73), and, in one version of the last known image of her, as a tough old widow in black, in about 1600, with a huge necklace of multiple rows of pearls (no. 9) A full-length of Mary, Queen of Scots (no. 11) was not there in Bess's day, and pays tribute to the romantic and erroneous 18th-century belief that she was imprisoned at Hardwick. Bess's granddaughter and ward Arbella Stuart, whose possible claim to the English crown brought much unhappiness to her short life, is painted full length in no. 1.

Furniture

The canopy halfway along the Gallery is one of the most magnificent examples of late 17th-century upholstery surviving in England. It had originally formed the tester and head of the bed in the state bedroom at Chatsworth supplied by Francis Lapierre in 1697. The 6th Duke installed it at Hardwick in the early 19th century as a piece of romantic stage scenery, for by his time canopies had no functional purpose in a private house. The decaying silk has recently been fully conserved as part of the English Heritage/HLF-funded programme of works.

Under the canopy now are two *high-backed chairs* of carved walnut with original red velvet upholstery appliquéd with silver thread, part of a set made about 1700 for the Queen of Scots' apartment at Chatsworth; five stools from the same suite are also in the Gallery. The whole set was brought over to Hardwick by the 6th Duke and originally placed in the High Great Chamber along with the Scots' apartment bed. Three of the richly carved feet from this demolished late 17th-century bed are displayed on the window ledge. Along the opposite wall is a set of late 17th-century *walnut armchairs* with high rectangular backs, and a set of circular and rectangular *walnut stools* of the same period; the *circular stools* have cushions with the remains of Elizabethan embroidery.

The long table in the north bay is covered with a late 16th-century Persian carpet, as Bess would have had it

Carpets

Two long tables in the room are covered by carpets in the Elizabethan manner. The great *carpet* of faded red and green silk enriched with gold and silver in the north bay is a Persian 16th-century carpet of the kind that excited the wonder and admiration of European travellers who visited the court of Shah Abbas at Isfahan. Although it was probably woven within a decade or two of the building of the house, it has been at Hardwick less than a hundred years.

The second *carpet* is a blue-ground Turkish medallion Ushak carpet and is one of the three Turkish carpets at Hardwick that may be survivors of the 32 mentioned in the 1601 inventory.

Metalwork

The two brass *chandeliers* are probably German or Flemish, late 16th- or early 17th-century.

Ceramics

On the table in the north-east alcove is a 15th-century *plate* of Hispano-Moresque lustre ware. On the inner wall is a selection of oriental porcelain *vases and jars* of the 17th and 18th centuries.

The Withdrawing Chamber

This room has gone through many changes. In Bess's time it rose as high as the High Great Chamber, but some time before 1764 the upper portion was cut off to make a room on the mezzanine floor, where the original stone cornice mouldings can still be seen. By then it had become a bedroom. The 6th Duke converted it into a library, and it was the room in which he mainly lived when at Hardwick. In the 20th century Duchess Evelyn took out the bookcases and made the room a state bed-chamber. It has now been restored as a withdrawing chamber, and the bed removed.

Overmantel

The alabaster overmantel carving of *Apollo and the Nine Muses*, with the royal arms and initials in the upper corners, was originally at Chatsworth and was probably made for the high great chamber there in the 1570s. The 6th Duke brought it to Hardwick. Apollo represented the rational, creative side of man's nature, here expressed in music, which would have played a large part in the entertainments at Hardwick.

Sea-dog table

The walnut table supported by chimeras or sea dogs resting on tortoises is perhaps the most important surviving piece of 16th-century furniture in England, of a regal quality which suggests it may originally have belonged to either Elizabeth or Mary and come to Bess as a gift. Similar beasts are shown on a state chair of Elizabeth's, as depicted in an engraving of 1575. It was in this room by 1601. Like the extravagantly pedimented walnut cupboard, it was based on engraved designs of about 1560 by the 16th-century French architect Du Cerceau.

1601 *The Withdrawing Chamber*

The hangings of classical heroines and their accompanying virtues, which are now in the Hall and on the Chapel landing, were in this room, with the Abraham tapestries, now in the Green Velvet Room, as an alternative set.

Tapestries

The present set of late 16th- or early 17th-century Flemish tapestries is thought to represent the story of Scipio or some other Roman general. The colours, unlike those in the Abraham tapestries next door, have faded, so that the reds have turned brown and fawn and the greens a soft blue.

Furniture

The room now contains most of the comparatively few pieces of Elizabethan furniture surviving at Hardwick. The more sumptuous pieces were either imported from abroad or made by foreign craftsmen working in London, and may have come to Chatsworth in the 1570s. The *cupboard* was probably one of the two 'cupboards guilt and carved with tills' ('tills' are drawers or compartments) in the High Great Chamber and Withdrawing Chamber.

A second, *smaller cupboard* decorated with Corinthian columns is also in the French manner, but in the more classical style associated with Jean Goujon; it retains more gilding than the other two pieces.

The *two-tier cabinet* with round-arched openings, also somewhat in the manner of Du Cerceau, might be somewhat inaccurately described as the 'cubberd guilt and inlayde with a marble stone in the side' in Arbella Stuart's chamber in 1601. The *square games table* inlaid with a board and playing cards is the only survivor of a number of inlaid tables listed in the 1601 inventory and is probably English work. The elaborate *marquetry chest* with arched panels in front inlaid with architectural scenes is in the German manner and has the initials GT inscribed on the keystones of the arches, probably standing for George or Gilbert Talbot.

Picture

Hanging on the north wall is *The return of Ulysses to Penelope*, 1570, which is one of the few non-portrait paintings in the house. Bess seems to have identified strongly with Penelope, the faithful wife who waits patiently the return of her husband from the Trojan Wars (by 1570 Bess's marriage to the Earl of Shrewsbury was already coming under strain). The weaving Penelope must also have appealed to a textile-lover like Bess. Alternatively, the picture may represent *Tarquinius Collatinus returning to Lucretia*, who was another classical exemplar of female virtue. The artist may be John Ballechouse, who was working at Chatsworth by 1578 and painted the wall-hangings in the Chapel at Hardwick (see p. 32).

(Right) The return of Ulysses to Penelope

(Above) The alabaster overmantel of Apollo and the Nine Muses was made for Elizabethan Chatsworth and brought here only in the 19th century

The Green Velvet Room

The elaborate *surround to the door and chimney-piece* is made of alabaster, blackstone and other Derbyshire marbles and was put up in 1599 by Thomas Accres, with the assistance of Henry Nayll and Richard Mallory; the little figure of Charity over the chimneypiece appears to be by the same sculptor as the overmantel figures in the Long Gallery.

Tapestries

The late 16th-century Flemish tapestries were the spare set of hangings for the Withdrawing Chamber in 1601; they were bought in London in 1592 from Sir William Hatton and his agent, and had belonged to Sir Christopher Hatton,

Elizabeth's dancing Lord Chancellor. Perhaps because they were not in regular use, they are still marvellously fresh in colour. They are a reduced and simplified version of the famous Abraham set of twelve pieces designed by Bernard Van Orley and woven by William Pannemaker of Brussels about 1540.

ANTI-CLOCKWISE FROM LEFT OF CHIMNEYPIECE:

Pharaoh returning Sarah to her husband Abraham

Abraham being offered bread and wine for his soldiers after the battle by the priest Melchisadek

Eliezer, Abraham's servant, being offered water to drink by Rebecca

Abraham entertaining the three angels who came to tell him of the destruction of Sodom and Gomorrah

(Above) Abraham being offered bread and wine by the priest Melchisadek; from the late 16th-century Flemish tapestries in the Green Velvet Room

Furniture

The splendid early 18th-century **green velvet bed** with matching chairs was brought by the 6th Duke from Londesborough and must originally have been made for the 3rd Earl of Burlington, whose daughter brought Londesborough, Chiswick, Bolton Abbey, Lismore Castle and other Burlington properties into the Devonshire family. The richly carved and gilt **stools**, *c.*1685, were originally in the state bedchamber at Chatsworth and were brought over to

Hardwick by the 6th Duke to accompany the tester of the Chatsworth state bed when he converted it into a canopy for the Long Gallery.

Picture

On the window wall is a copy of a self-portrait by Titian (*c.*1485–1576) with his friend, Andrea de' Franceschi, Grand Chancellor of Venice.

'This wilderness of a bedroom, with a quarry of marble in one corner.'

The 6th Duke

1601 The Best Bedchamber

The room was hung with seven embroidered hangings, including the three embroideries of the Virtues and their opposites, two of which are now in the Hall and the remains of the third (Hope and Judas) in store. It had an especially magnificent gilt bed with a valance of cloth of gold and silver, and blue and red curtains enriched with gold and silver trimmings.

The Mary, Queen of Scots Room

1601 *The Little Chamber within the Best Bedchamber*

Panelling

The woodwork in this room is very puzzling, and has provoked numerous theories. Over the door is a *semicircular panel* enclosing the Scottish royal arms and the initials MR and bordered with the inscription 'Marie Stewart par la grace de dieu reyne d'Ecosse douariere de France'. The style of the coat of arms is very similar to that on Mary's own seal, now in the British Museum, and there is no reason to suppose that it does not date from her time. Its history has never been established. It has been argued that it has always been in the room, but an alternative suggestion is that it came from the Queen of Scots' apartment at Chatsworth, and was brought to Hardwick when Chatsworth was being rebuilt; it may have been among the 'wainscot' sent to Hardwick in 1690.

In general, the *woodwork* seems much more elaborate than what is described in the 1601 inventory and seems to have been made up from

The making of a myth

The Shrewsburys were given the uncomfortable task of guarding the Queen's cousin and rival Mary, Queen of Scots from 1569 until her execution in 1587. Mary was held at Chatsworth and several of the Shrewsburys' many other houses, but never at Hardwick. Despite this, the legend grew up that she had been, and this room was created to satisfy the myth. It was reinforced by pictures like Laslett J. Pott's *Mary, Queen of Scots being led to her Execution* (illustrated here), which is set on the staircase at Hardwick (although her execution actually happened at Fotheringhay Castle in Northamptonshire).

(Above) The Mary, Queen of Scots Room in the 1820s; watercolour by William Hunt

a miscellany of sources. The door is dated 1599 and may be the original door made for the room. The little pedimented window looks at first sight to be 17th-century, but although the glazing bars may be of this date, the pediment is very similar to that on the Du Cerceau cupboard now in the Withdrawing Chamber and may have originated from Elizabethan Chatsworth.

Furniture

The *black velvet bed* is a much-restored version of one of the two beds which used to be shown as having belonged to Mary, Queen of Scots, and having been embroidered by her. There is no evidence and little likelihood of this. The bed may be a remake of the 'feild bedsted the postes being covered with black velvet' with hangings 'imbrodered with nedleworke flowers' which was in this room in 1601. The existing black velvet is 19th-century, but is mounted with early 17th-century flowers and borders.

The *black lacquer furniture* between the windows dates from the early 18th century; the four black lacquer chairs with matching day-bed are exceptionally early examples of japanning, probably dating from the 1660s.

Tapestries

The walls are hung with three pieces of Flemish verdure tapestry, probably early 17th century.

The Passage by the Mary, Queen of Scots Room

Needlework

This is hung with two sets of framed embroideries: a series of valances embroidered with signs of the zodiac set in fantastical landscapes; and a series of figures in appliqué work personifying the Liberal Arts bearing their symbols.

The Lobby between the Blue Room and the North Staircase

Panelling

The panelling over the door next to the stairs is decorated with engravings as in the High Great Chamber and was removed by the 6th Duke from over a door in the Dining Room. The other piece of panelling, painted with Hardwick and other arms, came from the Old Hall.

Pictures

The double-portrait over the door from the Queen of Scots Passage shows *Mary, Queen of Scots with her first husband, Lord Darnley*, whom she married in 1565. The marriage rapidly turned sour, and he was implicated in the murder of Mary's secretary Antonio Rizzio. Darnley was himself murdered in 1567. Bess married her daughter Elizabeth to Darnley's brother Charles Lennox – to the fury of Queen Elizabeth, whose permission was required (as Lennox had royal blood), but not asked. Bess brought up the only child of this marriage, Arbella Stuart, in the hope that she might succeed to the English throne after Elizabeth.

The Blue Room

The *cornice and doors* date from the late 17th century. The *chimneypiece* with its carved alabaster overmantel is probably the one brought to Hardwick from Chatsworth in 1691, when Chatsworth was being remodelled; if so, it probably dates from the 1570s. The cipher in the middle panel is made up of the initials E, G and M, presumably for Elizabeth and George Shrewsbury and Mary, Queen of Scots.

The Blue Room

Tapestries

The room is still hung with the four 'peeces of hanginges called the planetes' described in 1601. These are Brussels tapestries of the second half of the 16th century, and in fact depict a mixed set of gods and planets; prominent on the wall between the window and the door to Mary, Queen of Scots' Room is Neptune in a sea chariot, with Venus up in the sky in a chariot drawn by doves.

Furniture

The *bed* is based on one belonging to Christian Cavendish (née Bruce), wife of the 2nd Earl of Devonshire, and is embroidered with her arms and the date 1629, together with the arms of the 6th Duke and the date 1852. In the latter year the original embroidery was remounted on a new blue damask copying the original one.

The 18th-century *mahogany chairs* are covered with the same damask and mounted with 17th-century blue brocade *en suite* with that on the bed.

The *table* veneered with walnut 'oyster marquetry' and the matching torchère (the survivor of a pair) is early 18th-century, as are the other two torchères.

The *leather-covered chest* studded with brass nails and royal crowns and bearing the date 1727 may be one of two 'strong boxes' which, according to Lady Louisa Egerton were brought from Chiswick House in 1891.

The North Staircase

Each step is made of a single piece of oak. Look up to see the massive but simple joined construction of the staircase.

The Cut-Velvet Dressing Room

This part of the house underwent radical alteration in the late 17th century, when the recently elevated 1st Duke of Devonshire, busy rebuilding Chatsworth, also created two 'apartments', one at each end of the first floor of Hardwick for his wife and himself. The strange foliate carving issuing from a gnarled trunk that forms the door surrounds dates from this period, as does the panelling and the flossy-silk embroidered hangings. The overdoor paintings are of fantasy landscapes.

The Cut-Velvet Bedroom

1601 The Ship Bedchamber

Furniture

This room takes its name from the pink and green cut-velvet hangings on the *bed*, which was made about 1740 by Thomas Vardy. It was brought from Chatsworth by the 6th Duke.

At the foot of the bed is a large leather studded *blanket chest* of about 1730 with four crown straps up each front edge.

Tapestries

The two tapestries to the right as you enter the room depict events from the story of the Prodigal Son, while on the far wall is Cybele, from the set of Gods and Planets in the Blue Room. All three tapestries were made in Brussels in the late 16th century.

The Dining Room

1601 The Low Great Chamber

In 1601 this was richly and fully furnished for its various functions of sitting, eating and recreation, with a long table and cupboard for meals, two square tables for games and cards, pictures, curtains, eight tapestry hangings of the story of David and numerous richly trimmed and embroidered chairs, stools, forms and cushions.

Everything Elizabethan has since disappeared except for the *chimneypiece*, dated 1597, with its rather clumsy plasterwork overmantel and inscription 'The conclusion of all thinges is to feare God and keepe his commaundementes',

and the *wall sconces*, which may be the 'four plate Candlestickes of brass to hang on the wales' which were in the Hall in 1601; if so, one must be a later copy, for there are now five.

The room developed into a straightforward dining room and was slightly reduced in size in the late 17th century to enlarge the adjacent bedroom. The 6th Duke probably brought in the panelling from the Old Hall.

Furnishings

The furniture is mainly late 18th-century mahogany collected together from various places by Duchess Evelyn, who thought the room 'a more effective setting for plate and pretty clothes than the over-decorated dining room at Chatsworth'.

The mahogany *sideboard* is a later amalgamation of three late 18th-century pieces, a smaller sideboard and separate wine-cooler and knife-container in the form of urns on pedestals. The three *great brass dishes* are probably 17th-century. The blue-and-white *dinner service* carrying the Devonshire arms is a recent importation from Chatsworth and is probably Staffordshire ware of the early 19th century; although very decorative, it is not luxury ware and was probably originally made for use by the upper servants in the steward's room, or in the great dining room on public days.

In the bay there are a *grand piano* made by Broadwood in 1812 and a set of *virginals* by Thomas White, dated 1653.

Pictures

The room has been hung with 18th- and early 19th-century portraits of the Cavendishes and their relations since the time of the 6th Duke, who is depicted in one of the oval portraits on the south wall.

(Left) The Cut-Velvet Bedroom
(Right) The Dining Room

'Melancholy hooting'

As a boy the 6th Duke turned the deep window bay 'into a kind of menagerie: a fishing net nailed up under the curtain confined the rabbits, hedgehogs, squirrels, guinea pigs, and white mice, that were the joy of his life from 8 to 12 years old, the smell caused by these quadrupeds was overpowering. … A tree stood in the middle for the unhappy birds – caught by John Hall the gamekeeper – to perch on, and an owl made its melancholy hooting in one of the corners.' In later life he installed a billiard table … 'connected in this manner with an inhabited room, nothing in the world – no nothing can be more enjoyable'.

In the time of Duchess Evelyn, the recess was much used for the repair of tapestries, as it has the best light for this purpose in the house.

The Gallery

You can look down on the Entrance Hall from this gallery.

The Drawing Room

The room was used as a drawing room by Duchess Evelyn until 1959, and has been left largely as she furnished it, with family photographs, Chinese pottery and mainly 18th-century furniture.

The *panelling* probably comes from the Hill Great Chamber in the Old Hall. The Elizabethan *chimneypiece* is decorated with the Hardwick stags supporting the arms of Hardwick impaling an incorrectly repainted quartering.

Tapestries

These are the 'six pieces of tapestrie hanginges with personages and my Ladies Armes in them' in the room in 1601. They are Flemish, possibly of Oudenarde manufacture, dating from the second half of the 16th century, and their subject has still not been identified. Like the Gideon tapestries in the Long Gallery, they must have been bought from Sir William Hatton, as 'my Ladies Armes' were painted on pieces of cloth sewn over the Hatton arms; in all but one of the Drawing Room tapestries the Hardwick arms have been removed.

Embroideries

The framed panels showing *Europa and the Bull*, the *Death of Actaeon* and the *Fall of Phaeton* are embroidered with Bess's initials and were all originally cushion covers; in 1601 they were

(Right) The Drawing Room

in the Best Bedchamber, Long Gallery and Withdrawing Chamber.

Furniture and ceramics

The early 18th-century Dutch *marquetry cabinet* houses a collection of blue-and-white china, prominent in which is a *Ming porcelain jug* with Elizabethan silver-gilt mounts dated 1589.

The four 18th-century *chairs* to either side of the cabinet have cross-stitch covers worked by Duchess Evelyn.

Pictures

The portraits include Henry VIII about 1536, shortly before he grew a beard, and his son, Edward VI. Also hanging here are Mary, Queen of Scots, her husband Lord Darnley and their niece, Arbella Stuart aged 23 months, holding a doll in full Elizabethan dress. The infant is described by the inscription as Countess of Lennox, and sports a small shield decorated with a countess's coronet. This is in allusion to her claim to succeed to the Scottish earldom and lands of Lennox, which were unjustly, in her grandmother's view, purloined by her cousin King James.

The Drawing Room Passage

1601 *At My Lady's Chamber Door*

You leave by a passage that separated the Drawing Room from Bess's Bedchamber.

Canvas-work

Here are displayed 32 octagonal canvas-work panels reproducing designs from 16th-century botanical plate-books and bordered with mottos. Panels like these (many bear Bess's monogram) are also incorporated in the celebrated hangings now at Oxburgh Hall, Norfolk, which are known to have been worked on by Bess and Mary, Queen of Scots. The other screens contain small panels of personifications, including virtues and vices, nymphs and goddesses. These were probably originally part of the Best Bed hangings recorded in the 1601 inventory. They were mounted in glazed screens by Duchess Evelyn.

Pictures

The portraits are mainly of 18th- and 19th-century Cavendishes.

Furniture

The heraldic inlaid *table* on a later stand is probably one of the 'inlaide bordes' mentioned in the 1601 inventory.

Retrace your steps across the Gallery to reach the Paved Room.

The octagonal canvas-work panels in the Drawing Room Passage are based on engravings in a contemporary herbal

The Paved Room

As this room was originally intended to be the first-floor landing of the Staircase, it has stone paving like the staircase landings elsewhere in the house, instead of being plastered for rush matting like the other rooms. Its modest furnishings suggest that it was used as a dining room by the upper servants. By the early 20th century it had become a bedroom.

The handsome *overmantel plaster relief* shows the earth-goddess Cybele, and derives in effectively simplified form from an engraving after Hendrick Goltzius. The date 1588 in the plasterwork may be an ignorant repainting of the original date (1598), which had been defaced, but it is possible that it has been moved in from elsewhere, perhaps from the Old Hall.

Furniture

The late 18th-century *bed* is hung with cream cotton embroidered with coral-pink arabesques.

The Chapel

The Chapel was originally on two levels, in the usual manner of chapels in big country houses, with the family and their guests in an upper gallery, looking down on a lower chapel for the servants. The lower chapel was shut off by the 5th Duke to make a steward's room for the upper servants; by 1800 these were no longer gentlemen and gentlewomen, but they were still accustomed to live in some style and be waited on by the lower servants. The exact original size and arrangement of the upper chapel are uncertain. The present *communion rails* have been made up, probably in the 19th century, from a miscellany of original panelling. The *pulpit* was brought up from the lower chapel and is probably 17th-century.

Wall-hangings

'The English make such use of … painted cloths which are very well executed … for there are few houses you could enter without finding these.'

Etienne Perlin, 1558

The four wall-hangings, painted with scenes from the life of St Paul and with the Hardwick arms, are not identifiable in the 1601 inventory, but may be those for which the French painter John Ballechouse was paid in 1599–1600. Such painted cloths were an alternative to tapestry, the style of which they imitated; they were common in the 16th century, but the Hardwick ones are among only a very few that have survived.

(Left) The plaster relief of the earth-goddess Cybele in the Paved Room

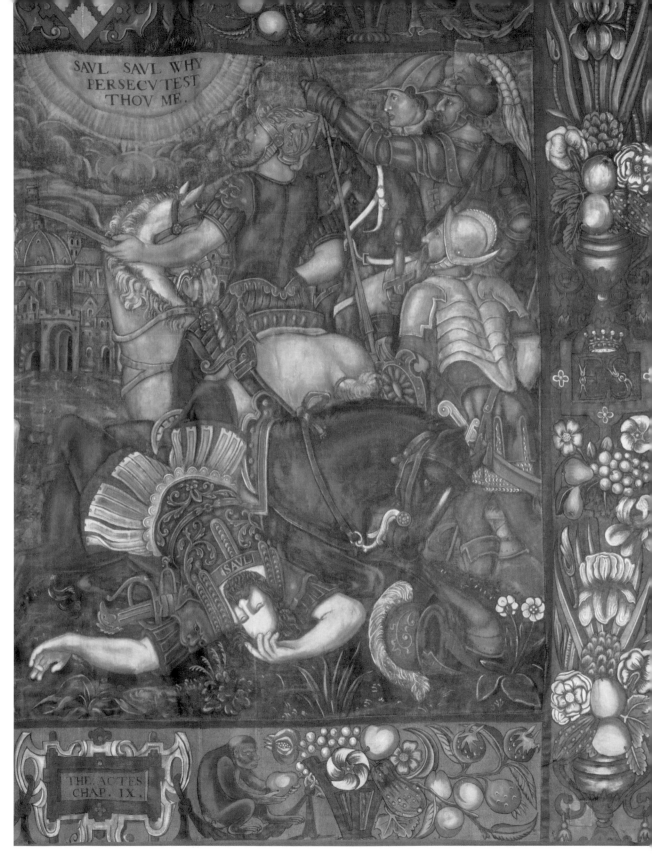

The rare painted wall-hangings in the Chapel depict the life of St Paul

The embroidered hanging of Zenobia on the Chapel Stairs

The Chapel Stairs and Landing

The two stone *doorcases* were carved in 1596; the one leading to the wooden stairs is by William Griffin and James Adams, and the other, to the Paved Room, is by Henry Nayl and Richard Mallery. Neither ever had more than one pilaster. The splendid *plasterwork cartouches enclosing heads* are in the same style as that over the door to the Drawing Room.

The hanging *lantern* on the landing is probably the 'great glass Lanthorne' of the 1601 inventory.

Furniture

The big oak *chest* by the chapel screen conceals a hot plate for the Dining Room, installed by Duchess Evelyn.

Embroideries

The two *embroidered hangings* of Zenobia with Magnanimity and Prudence, and Artemisia with Piety (filial piety) and Constancy, are part of the same series as the two in the Hall, and were originally in the Withdrawing Chamber. The Artemisia hanging is dated 1573; Piety is exemplified by the Athenian Pero breast-feeding her father through the bars of his prison cell.

Panelling

The four *intarsia panels* of stained and inlaid wood depicting architectural perspectives were brought over by the 6th Duke from the Old Hall; one of them is dated 1576 and there is little doubt that they were originally at Chatsworth, where many of the rooms in the Elizabethan house were lined with inlaid panelling. The Staircase panels, which are based on engravings, are remarkable examples of direct Renaissance influence in Elizabethan England.

The Kitchen

Food and drink consumed at Hardwick during the New Year festivities, 26 December to 1 January 1668–9	
71 beefs	7 plovers
180 muttons	4 str apples
51 veals	18 geese
1 calfs head	11 partridges
22 tongues	30 woodcocks
1 capon	4 barrels oysters
57 pullets	10 pigs
16 chickens	10 turkeys
98 rabbits	6 brawns
3/4 venison	9 widgeons
32 porks	2 peewits (?)
1 grenfish (?)	10 hogshead small beer
5 carps	2 hogshead strong beer
2 pike	5 hogshead small ale
32 bacons	34 quarts sherry
251 butters	19 quarts celery wine
1500 eggs	30 quarts claret
6 cheeses	30 quarts white wine
22 gallons cream	
Provisions book of the 3rd Earl of Devonshire	

In Elizabethan times cooking was done at huge open fires in the kitchen, except for baking, which took place in brick-lined ovens in the pantry, a separate room in the north turret. A serving hatch connected the Kitchen with the original serving room, which has long been joined with the pantry (now the shop).

Open fires continued to be used until the 19th century, and over one of the fireplace arches is fixed a late 18th-century brass and iron bracket for supporting spits. In the late 17th century a crude precursor of the kitchen range, known as a *stewing hearth*, began to be used, and there is a rare survivor of one of these, probably installed in the 18th century, under the kitchen window. It consists of a series of plates, each of which was heated separately by charcoal placed in an arched recess without a flue.

The stewing hearth gradually developed into the one-fire closed *Victorian cast-iron range*, and two of these were fitted into the original Elizabethan chimney opening.

1601 The Kitchen

The kitchen equipment consisted of copper and brass pans, a brass kettle, a brass pestle and mortar, a frying pan, a chopping knife, a mincing knife, a cleaver, a gridiron, a grater, ten spits, five dripping pans, a skimmer and a hatchet.

Furnishings

The robustly solid kitchen *furniture* was probably installed by the 6th Duke; the splendid collection of *copper kitchen utensils*, all engraved with the Devonshire crest or arms, dates from the 18th and 19th centuries. The *hatchment* bears the arms of the 6th Duke, and was painted for his funeral in 1858.

The gardens

The arrangement of courts and orchards around the New Hall is contemporary with the building of the house, and they form an integral part of the design. Like the house, they are symmetrical, apart from the truncation of the North Orchard due to the lie of the land. Although the grounds are spacious – eleven acres in all – they were not always elaborate and have not always been meticulously kept.

In the mid-17th century, the gardener was 'old John Booth', who came over from Edensor armed with spade, rake and hoe to maintain the fruit and vegetables in the kitchen garden. Although he was not resident, he had several labourers at his command, including a local housewife to do the weeding. As well as the kitchen garden, the other plots were often functional rather than decorative, providing pasture for animals, with the grass grown long for hay in places, giving the Hall a rustic look.

In the 1660s a more ornamental approach was taken, with the elm walk planted in the 'Laund', 'a gravell walk in Hardwick garden for my lady to walke out on' replacing a turf alley, and fruit trees planted in the West Court.

The outlines of the present gardens are still dictated by the 17th-century layout, but it was the developments of the 19th and early 20th centuries that produced its present character.

The garden contains something of interest throughout the year. Spring bulbs and fruit blossom are followed by roses in the East Court and New Orchard and summer flowers in the long South Orchard border. The Herb Garden is at its best throughout the summer, while the West Court borders are most colourful in late summer and autumn.

The West Court

The original layout was simple, with paving down the centre. Fruit trees were planted in 1669. In 1833 the court was laid out as an elaborate flower garden by Blanche, the 6th Duke's niece, with a design centred on two beds in the shape of an E and an S, echoing Bess's initials on the parapets of the house, surrounded by circular beds, scrolls and borders. Plants originally included dahlias, lilac, laurel, roses, rhododendrons, heather and brooms. All this was swept away after the First World War, and the court was turfed over.

The much-worn stone drums, carved with ox-skulls and festoons, to the left and right of the colonnade, were originally part of a set of four, drawn by S. H. Grimm in 1785 as central features of the lawn in the East Court. Such drums were inspired by the pedestals supporting Roman statues; the Hardwick drums may originally also have been pedestals for statues and perhaps date from the mid-17th century.

The borders are planted in rich colours, using the sort of graded colour scheme favoured by Gertrude Jekyll.

The East Court

The East Court with its four yews was until recently plain green, a prelude to a view out over the ha-ha to the avenue of limes starting in an amphitheatre across the park, planted in 1930. The piers of the gateways probably date from 1686. The pond in the centre was made in 1920 as a fire-fighting reservoir. The green was enlivened by the introduction, in about 1950, of old roses that would tolerate the shade of the trees and the northerly aspect, with an underplanting of ground-cover plants such as bergenias and pulmonarias.

The South Orchard

In the 17th century, this area was planted with fruit trees, and was probably also the site of the kitchen garden, as it was until the 20th century. Today, it is divided into four quarters by hedged alleys of yew and hornbeam. This layout was devised by Lady Louisa Egerton, daughter of the 7th Duke, in 1861, incorporating lead statues brought over from Londesborough.

(Above) The herbaceous border in the West Court

The herb garden created by the National Trust in the 1960s occupies the south-western quarter. The plants are predominantly those that would have been familiar to an Elizabethan household. Next to it is a nuttery with walnuts, cobs and filberts, underplanted with naturalised spring flowers.

The two eastern quarters are occupied by orchards. The more formal, productive one to the south (the New Orchard) is planted with old varieties of apples, pears, plums, gages and damsons and has a border of old roses, clematis and tulips in the spring planted against a back-cloth of the yew hedge. The second orchard, next to the house, has pears and ornamental crab apples more spaciously planted and in spring and early summer is treated as a wild garden, with mown paths through long grass containing naturalised bulbs.

The character of the north-west quarter, in contrast to both orchards and herb garden, is of a broad expanse of green lawn planted informally with specimen trees. In 1995 the 11th Duke of Devonshire planted a *Fraxinus excelsior* 'Jaspidea' in honour of the Trust's centenary, and in 1997 Queen Elizabeth II planted a *Phillyrea latifolia* during her visit to celebrate Hardwick's 400th anniversary.

Beyond the herb garden are nursery plots for growing cut flowers and vegetables for the house, and a mulberry walk planted by the National Trust. At its southern end is an Elizabethan banqueting house, which was occasionally used by the 6th Duke's private orchestra as a smoking room, since they were not allowed to smoke in the house.

Lady Spencer's Walk

This woodland walk was created in 1797 by Georgiana, Countess Spencer, the mother-in-law of the 5th Duke, and eventually the whole wood came to bear her name. Originally, the walk consisted of a gravelled path through the middle of the plantation with a loop at each end. Some time in the early 19th century, the walk was extended further east to a small valley known as Hollowdale and later, in 1844, into Hollowdale itself.

Following the First World War the wood gradually returned to an uncultivated state, but has recently been restored.

The estate and park

The name Hardwick means 'sheep farm', a clue to the hilly and wooded pastureland on which it is situated. However, to the south and west of the present house there is some evidence of ridge and furrow on the steep banks, accompanied by small settlements, which suggests that in places the land was ploughed, probably in the 13th century.

When Bess's grandfather, John Hardwick, died in 1507, he left an estate of 400 acres in and around Hardwick. But the next years were to be hard ones for the family fortunes. Bess's father died young in 1528, leaving his only son, James, a minor less than two years old, so that the estate was taken into wardship for nearly twenty years. Once James inherited, he managed to lose heavily by foolish speculation, dying bankrupt in the Fleet Prison in London in 1581.

Feckless James was succeeded by his sister Bess, who, in contrast, was a hard-headed businesswoman, wise in her investments, and tough in her bargains. Even so, she had a hard time raising the capital to buy Hardwick, complaining that her husband, the Earl of Shrewsbury, 'would not give her money to purchase the land of Hardwick her brother deceased'. Nevertheless, on 2 June 1583, she bought Hardwick outright for £9,500 for her favourite son, William Cavendish.

William Senior's survey, 1609–10

The best record of the Elizabethan estate is the volume of plans made in 1609–10 for William Cavendish by William Senior, now preserved at Chatsworth. Senior's maps show that enclosures were already taking place, especially in Hardstoft. Early enclosure was piecemeal, strips of ridge and furrow being taken in bit by bit. This was reflected in the sinuous shapes of the fields in the 19th century, and remains apparent to a much reduced extent today. Later geometric enclosures of the 18th and 19th centuries, having less regard for the lie of the land, form a marked contrast with their predecessors.

Hardwick stands out in Senior's plans as being quite different from the other parts of the parish. The park is boldly delineated and the manor is largely given over to woodland and pasture, with no village and no field system. Nothing is known of the park at Hardwick before a survey made by James Hardwick in 1570, although the evidence of deserted settlements and ridge and furrow suggests that it was not emparked until after the 13th century.

Senior's map shows the park divided into two, respecting the natural differences between its eastern and western parts. The western, larger part was typical of medieval parks, with tree-clothed banks intersected by watercourses. The hilly land there was favoured by the oak trees for which Hardwick park was famous.

The eastern part of the park overlies a limestone plateau on which ash grows best. The land here was called the 'lawnd' or lawn, signifying a flattish grassy area with a sparser tree cover. It was fenced off separately and was ploughed occasionally in the 17th century. Its topography rendered it the most suitable part of the park for a formal arrangement of trees, and in the 17th century an elm walk was planted there, probably in or around 1656. It does not appear to have been a success and was removed in 1730.

Expansion and decline

In 1665 the park was greatly expanded by the addition of part of Rowthorne Carr and by the purchase from the Molyneux family of some emparked land in the neighbouring parish of Teversal. This land, consisting of banks of old trees, fish-ponds, woodland pasture and a small deer-park, was known as 'New Parke'. By this period, however, the Cavendishes had come to prefer Chatsworth, and expenditure on Hardwick was meagre in comparison. The Old Hall became superfluous, and in 1747–57 the eastern part was demolished. The south elevation, however, was saved, possibly for its picturesque effect.

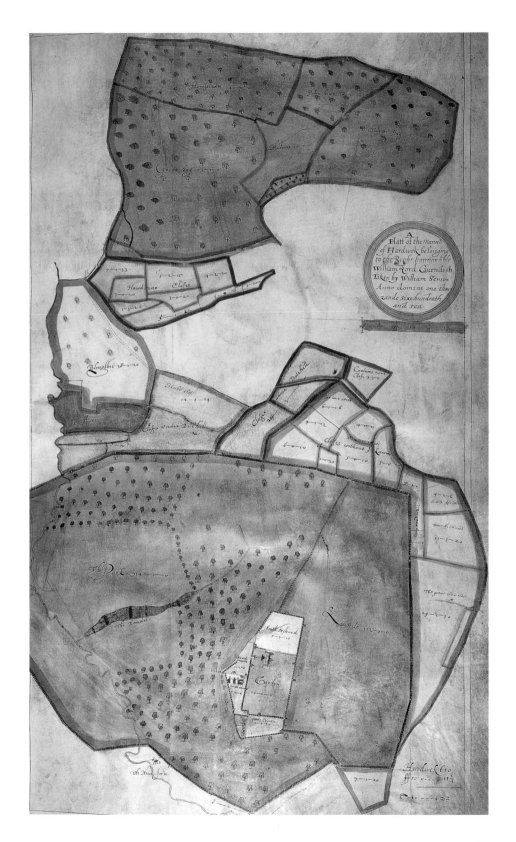

*William Senior's
1609–10 survey
of the estate*

Revival

By the end of the 18th century, the Baroque glories of Chatsworth seemed passé, and the Cavendishes showed renewed interest in Hardwick.

The Bachelor Duke carried out some important changes in the park. In 1822–4 he made new drives through the park to Glapwell Gate and Blingsby Gate. These drives were bordered by 'clump avenues' of oak trees, normally called the 'Platoons' because of their likeness to groups of soldiers. Some time before 1855, bare areas in the park were filled with a group of small circular and oval plantations.

In the years immediately following the 6th Duke's death in 1858, several ambitious improvements took place at Hardwick. Thomas Crump of Derby was commissioned in 1859 to install a steam engine to pump water up to the house and offices; the engine house, with a detached, tall stone chimney, still survives in the park (and now houses the Stone Centre, where visitors can discover more about the use of stone and the stone-mason's art). The stables were completely overhauled and a new servants' wing was built at the north end of the Hall. Work of an equally extensive nature took place at the Great Ponds, which were remodelled and cleaned in 1857–61. This work necessarily damaged the natural marshy habitat for wildfowl, so in 1860 a duck decoy was built to compensate for the loss.

The extensive work at the New Hall, in the park and on the estate generally was mirrored in the growth of the estate buildings on the hillside below the Stableyard, near Crump's Engine House. A sawmill was built there in 1861, and a new mason's shed, lime house and mess room were built in 1879. But by the 1870s the pace of developments was slowing down; Carr Plantation was planted in 1870, and Norwood Lodge was built in 1874, but the proposed lodges at Blingsby Gate and Gin Gate were never built. Life at Hardwick appears to have become uneventful, but the park was probably at its best in the 1870s, and there was little substantial change until the First World War.

Cutting back

The economic difficulties brought about by the First World War meant reduction rather than improvement. The gardens could no longer be cultivated to the same extent, Lady Spencer's Walk was neglected, and the flower-beds in the West Court were turfed over. In the park, the deer were gradually phased out, and much of the former grassland in the eastern part of the park was put under the plough. Timber shortage was another problem, as the best timber had been removed in the First World War.

Nevertheless, the lime avenue was planted in 1926–7, possibly on the site of the 17th-century elm walk. Because of its shape it is known as the Wine Glass. Over half a mile long, the avenue makes good use of the terrain and available space to obtain the best possible effect. It was the idea of Duchess Evelyn, who was passionately interested in the trees at Hardwick.

Hardwick at war

At the outbreak of the Second World War, parts of the park were given over to the army and the RAF. Despite the unsuitable terrain, the land on top of the limestone ridge was requisitioned by the RAF for a landing strip, which entailed tearing down part of Duchess Evelyn's lime walk. The 1st Parachute Brigade was formed at Hardwick in 1941. For the remainder of the war Hardwick was the depot and School of Airborne Forces, where volunteers from all ranks of the army went through selection tests and received their specialised training. Every airborne participant in the Normandy invasion, whether by parachute or glider, went through initial training at Hardwick.

Bicycle thieves
When Millers Pond was dredged in the 1970s, some 600 bicycles were recovered from the silt. They had been dumped there out of sight, having been commandeered by the troops on nights out in nearby towns after they had missed the transport back to camp.

Hardwick park
and surrounding area

☐ Area outside parts of park
open to visitors

N ←

To
Newbound
Mill

Norwood

Carr
Plantation

Norwood
Lodge

Windnook
Gate

Carr
Ponds

County
Dumble

Park
Spring

Slack
Lodge
site of

Park
Farm

Lodge

Griff
Wood

Park
Piece

County
Boundary

Lady
Spencer's
Wood

Lodge
Plantation

Glapwell
Gate

Ault
Hucknall

Church

Breedon
Close
Gate

The
"Wineglass"

Dovedale
Wood

Hosp.

Randall
Gate

Stableyard

Horse
Pasture

Cross
Wood

The
Grange

New Hall

Hucknall
Wood

? Site
of
Bole

HARDWICK
PARK

Top
Quarry

Old
Hall

Kennels

Hodmire
Closes

Broadoak
Hill

Mill
Farm

Stainsby Park

Blingsby
Gate

Miller's Pond
Roundels

Military Camp
site of

Inn

Decoy

Lower
Quarry

Great
Pond

Stainsby Mill

Blingsby

River Doe Lea

Junction 29

To
Heath

Manor
House
(site of)

Junction 28

Stainsby
School

Motorway M1
opened 1967

STAINSBY

Stainsby
Pond

To
Astwith

To
Hardstoft

The National Trust

Hardwick Hall came to the National Trust with 1,000 acres of adjacent park and woodland. Under the Countryside Act of 1968, the western part of the park was converted into a Country Park during the 1970s, allowing the clearing and restoration of the Great and Row ponds, the provision of footpaths, facilities for angling, and the building of a modest visitor information centre. This centre was enlarged in 2004 and is now the base for the National Trust's team of wardens.

When the Trust took over Hardwick, it found that the park had been badly damaged by the dairy farming, so it seemed sensible to stock it with animals appropriate to the area, interesting to look at, and which would contribute to the preservation of breeds in danger of extinction. Choice was not difficult: longhorn cattle, which once dominated the rural scene, had been developed 200 years ago by the great breeder Robert Bakewell, 30 miles away in Leicestershire. In addition a breed of sheep, White Faced Woodland, from the Peak District estates of the Devonshires was introduced.

Hardwick Inn

Situated at one of the southern park entrances, it was designed and built in 1608 by the painter John Ballechouse (see p. 56) as his own residence. The house was originally T-shaped, impressive and spacious, but it is interesting that Ballechouse, in spite of his knowledge of contemporary design and decoration, chose the local vernacular style for his own house.

John was succeeded by his son James, who served as 'receiver' for the estate. An inventory made in February 1647/8 provides a fascinating insight into the appearance of the inn. It was furnished with 'Bedding furniture etc., fitting for the entertainment of gentlemen and strangers', and was certainly comfortable by the

standards of the time. The Dining Parlour, having a long table with a side form, fifteen covered stools and six other seats, was designed to take a lot of people. It was made more relaxing by cushions, carpets, curtains, a glass lantern and '3 great pictures'. The Hall, more spartanly furnished with trestles, forms and stools, was evidently the bar. There was a brew-house at the inn with a mash vat, and down in the cellars were a great brewing vat, six hogsheads, barrels and 'other wooden ware'. Upstairs, there were eight chambers, the kitchen chamber being lavishly and extravagantly decked out in blue, yellow and black fabrics. Books at the inn in 1648 included popular literature such as 'Smith's Sermons', 'ye practice of pietie', 'the book of Martiers [Foxe]', and a Bible.

Throughout the 17th and 18th centuries, upper servants from the New Hall lived at the inn. It was restored and re-roofed in 1852–3, and possibly partially rebuilt.

Stableyard buildings

On the brink of a steep slope forming the edge of the limestone plateau stands the west range, consisting of brew-house, wash-house and dairy, built between 1589 and 1591. Brewing continued until 1857, and the brew-house was converted into a house for the gardener in 1872. Today, the west range is a mixture of staff accommodation and holiday cottages.

Senior's plan of 1609–10 shows no buildings on the south side apart from a smithy, which still stands. By the mid-17th century it was joined by a slated great barn, which in the 20th century was divided into a fire-engine shed, garages and a cowshed. The original form is nevertheless still discernible: open end-to-end, roof-to-floor with a threshing floor in the middle flanked by large doors.

In 1858–61 the stableyard buildings were repaired and altered, with the addition of a wagon-shed, and a clock and bell turret erected on the great barn.

Stainsby Mill

There has been a watermill at Stainsby since the 13th century, probably on the same site as the present one, which is shown on Senior's plan. It passed to Bess of Hardwick with her purchase of the manor of Stainsby in 1593, and from the mid-17th century until its closure in the 1940s it was worked as part of Stainsby Mill Farm.

The mill dam at Stainsby was insufficient to power the mill: additional water was obtained from Millers Pond in Hardwick Park, and from Stainsby Pond, which was built in 1762 solely for the purpose of supplying the mill with water.

Following a period of disrepair in the 1840s, the building was completely reconstructed in 1849–50 and fitted with new machinery supplied by Kirkland & Son of Mansfield. The machinery is still remarkably complete and includes a kiln, drying floor, three pairs of stones and an iron waterwheel 1.5 metres wide and 5.2 metres in diameter. The mill has been repaired by the National Trust and is open to the public.

(Left) Hardwick Inn
(Right) Stainsby Mill

Bess of Hardwick

Bess of Hardwick's nickname ties her securely to the house she built. So do her initials, with which she decorated its skyline, and her coat of arms, which she scattered profusely over its interiors. There is probably no other house in England which is so closely connected in popular imagination with one person. And she was a person to be reckoned with.

Bess was born at Hardwick in about 1527, one of a family of four girls and a boy. The Hardwicks were minor gentry who had been established at Hardwick for at least six generations. They owned a few hundred acres and lived in a small manor house on the site of Hardwick Old Hall. Bess's father died in 1528, leaving each of his daughters £26 13s 4d. By the 1540s Bess had gone into service in the household of a neighbouring great Derbyshire family, that of Sir John Zouche of Codnor Castle.

A step upwards
First marriage: to Robert Barlow

To be a gentlewoman or upper servant in a big household was an accepted course for the children of the Tudor gentry. It was a form of practical education and a useful step towards marriage. In about 1543 Bess married her cousin Robert Barlow, heir of a Derbyshire gentry family slightly more prosperous than the Hardwicks. The circumstances of the marriage are somewhat mysterious. She is said to have looked after him when he was sick in the Zouche house in London, where he was probably also a member of the household. He died a few months after the marriage, 'before they were bedded' according to one account. She received the customary widow's jointure, probably of a third of his

income. By 1588 this amounted to £66 a year, a comfortable little sum by contemporary money values, but certainly not a fortune. As a childless widow she probably continued to serve in great households, and may have become one of the gentlewomen of the Marchioness of Dorset, the mother of Lady Jane Grey. This would explain why her second marriage, to Sir William Cavendish, took place in the Grey family chapel at Bradgate Manor in Leicestershire.

Founding three dukedoms
Second marriage: to Sir William Cavendish

Her second marriage, which took place in 1547, brought her a notable increase in status. Sir William Cavendish was an elderly, distinguished and extremely rich government servant, already

(Right) Although inscribed as of Queen Mary, this is probably a portrait of Bess around 1557, when she was 30 and married to Sir William Cavendish

Sir William Cavendish, Bess's second husband, about 1550

twice married, with two surviving daughters but no son. He was a typical example of the new men who made their fortune under the Tudors. He had been one of the commissioners for the Dissolution of the Monasteries and in 1546 had bought the lucrative office of Treasurer of the Chamber. In the course of his career he had picked up considerable property, widely scattered over five counties. According to the Duchess of Newcastle (who married Bess's grandson in the mid-17th century) 'being somewhat advanced in years, he married her chiefly for her beauty'. To please his new wife he sold all his existing property and bought new property in Derbyshire and Nottinghamshire. Among his purchases were the house and estate of Chatsworth, which he bought in 1549. Up till 1547 these had belonged to Francis Leche, who was both Bess of Hardwick's step-brother and brother-in-law. The Cavendishes pulled down the existing house and started to build a new one, on the site of the Chatsworth of today.

Bess's Cavendish marriage was not the longest lasting of her marriages but it was much the most successful and the only one which produced children – eight children, of whom three sons and three daughters survived infancy. Her eldest son Henry had no legitimate children (though described by a contemporary as 'the common bull to all Derbyshire and Staffordshire'); from her second son William descended the Cavendishes, Dukes of Devonshire, of Chatsworth and Hardwick, and from her third son Charles, the Cavendishes, Dukes of Newcastle, and Cavendish-Bentincks, Dukes of Portland, of Welbeck and Bolsover. The foundations of these dukedoms were laid by Bess.

The fruits of ambition

With her second marriage Bess emerged from obscurity, and the main aspects of her character became clear. She was capable, managing, acquisitive, a businesswoman, a money-maker, a land-amasser, a builder of great houses, an indefatigable collector of the trappings of wealth and power, and inordinately ambitious, both for herself and her children. She wrote in a clear Renaissance hand, and the wealth of classical imagery in the decoration and architecture of her houses suggests a cultivated woman; but her biographers have been puzzled by the fact that only six books are listed in the 1601 inventory. She was immensely tough, but it would be a mistake to think of her as either cold or calculating. She was capricious, rash, emotional, fond of intrigue and gossip, easily moved to tears, the best of company when things were going her way and spitting with spite and fury when crossed. Her amazing vitality carried her unflaggingly through her four marriages and widowhood to her death in her eighties, immensely rich and still formidable. Her unrelenting acquisition of property and worldly goods, especially of property in the countryside of her birth, and if possible connected with her family and relatives, suggests the ambition of a local girl to demonstrate that the dim squire's daughter had made good in a sensational way.

A place at court
Third marriage: to Sir William St Loe

William Cavendish died in 1557, leaving her with a life interest in Chatsworth and in a substantial proportion of his property. Two years later she was married again, to a rich West Country landowner, Sir William St Loe. Like William Cavendish, he had already been twice married and had daughters. Socially the marriage was yet another step up for Bess, for the St Loes were an older and better-established family than the Cavendishes, and Sir William held the post of Captain of the Guard and Butler of the Royal Household and was a favourite courtier of the Queen's. The marriage lasted only five years; he died in the winter of 1564–5, leaving much of his property outright to Bess, to the indignation of his family. She was on the marriage market again and now a formidable prize. There was much gossip as to whom she would marry next.

George, 6th Earl of Shrewsbury, Bess's fourth husband

Wealth and position
Fourth marriage: to the Earl of Shrewsbury

Her catch, in the end, was a sensational one. In 1567 she married George Talbot, 6th Earl of Shrewsbury, a widower with six children. He was 40, head of one of the oldest, grandest and richest families in England. By the side of his formidable wife he tends to seem rather a colourless character, but it would be a mistake to underrate him. He used his inherited wealth as a basis on which he became perhaps the biggest tycoon in England. He was a farmer on a vast scale, an exploiter of coal-mines and glassworks, an ironmaster and shipowner with interests in lead and steel. The main part of his properties was in the Midlands, like those of his new wife. The deal was clinched by a triple marriage; not only did Lord Shrewsbury marry Bess, but his second son married her daughter Mary, and his daughter married her eldest son Henry.

Dangerous relations

Within two years Lord Shrewsbury was saddled with an important, but unenviable assignment. Early in 1569 he was given the custody of Mary, Queen of Scots, who had fled across the border to England in May 1568. He remained her custodian until 1584. She moved between his many houses: Tutbury Castle, Sheffield Castle, Sheffield Manor, Wingfield Manor, Worksop Manor, his lodge at Buxton and his wife's house at Chatsworth. In spite of later legend, there is no evidence or likelihood that she was ever at Hardwick.

In 1574 Bess, probably on the spur of the moment, compromised her daughter Elizabeth with Charles Stuart, the brother of Mary, Queen of Scots' ex-husband Lord Darnley. A hurried marriage was arranged between them. Any child of Charles Stuart had a claim to the succession after the death of Elizabeth. The chance of having descendants on the English throne was too tempting for Bess to ignore, but in the long run the marriage brought her nothing but trouble. Queen Elizabeth was justifiably furious, and Charles Stuart's mother spent the winter of 1574–5 imprisoned in the Tower of London. A daughter, Arbella Stuart, born in 1575, was the only child of the marriage; both parents died within a few years, leaving Bess as Arbella's guardian.

A marriage in ruins

The Stuart marriage took place without Lord Shrewsbury's knowledge or approval, and it must have seemed to him that his wife was risking his good relations with the Queen for the sake of her own family. Their marriage began to run into trouble. Another subject of contention was Chatsworth, which Bess was now remodelling on a magnificent scale, and which her husband thought took up a disproportionate amount of her time and interest, and his own money. But

Mary, Queen of Scots with her husband, Lord Darnley. The Shrewsburys had the uncomfortable task of guarding Mary during her imprisonment

probably the main source of strain was Mary, Queen of Scots, who inevitably became a centre of intrigue on a European scale, so that the Shrewsburys lived in a state of constant tension. They had their first serious row in 1577. In 1584 the marriage broke down completely, and, in spite of constant efforts by Elizabeth and the Privy Council, it was never properly patched up.

The collapse of the marriage had important consequences for Hardwick. In about 1583 Bess bought the house and property from the estate of her brother James, who had been heavily in debt for many years. When the quarrel between her and her husband broke out, one of the bones of contention was Chatsworth, which Lord Shrewsbury claimed belonged to him under the terms of their marriage settlement, and attempted to occupy by force. It remained a subject of dispute for several years, and although Shrewsbury was ordered by the Privy Council to allow her one of his own houses to live in, he made life as difficult as possible for her. Bess accordingly concentrated on her own undisputed property at Hardwick and between about 1585 and 1590 enlarged and remodelled the old house to become what is now known as Hardwick Old Hall.

Arbella Stuart at two. Bess's granddaughter had a claim to the English throne through her father, the Earl of Lennox – a claim that may have encouraged Bess to build Hardwick

A birthplace transformed

Lord Shrewsbury died in 1590. For some years he had been living with his mistress in a small house outside Sheffield. Bess now recovered complete control of all her lands with a very large widow's jointure in addition. She was in her early sixties, and one of the richest people in England. Immediately after her husband's death, or possibly even a few weeks before it, she laid out the foundations of a new, larger and grander house a few yards away from the still uncompleted Hardwick Old Hall. Hardwick, rather than Chatsworth, became her principal home, perhaps because it was her own property and the place where she had been born, whereas she only had a life interest in Chatsworth. After her death it would go to her eldest son Henry, who had taken her husband's side in the quarrel, and whom she heartily disliked; Hardwick, on the other hand, was destined for her favourite son, William.

The next thirteen years were spent in building and furnishing Hardwick, in running her properties, making money, buying even more land for herself and her sons, and coping with the increasing problem of Arbella. The pretty bright-eyed baby shown in the portrait in the Drawing Room at Hardwick had grown into a spoilt and lively girl who was well aware that many people were betting on her chances of being the next queen of England. She became the centre of numerous intrigues, mostly concerned with

(Right) Arbella Stuart aged thirteen. She was brought up at Hardwick, but came to hate Bess

marrying her to various important people. Queen Elizabeth played her usual game of refusing to commit herself; she checkmated all marriage plans and showed no signs of declaring Arbella or anyone else her heir. Arbella paid occasional visits to court, but mostly she was made to live safely out of the way at Hardwick. Her grandmother was by now too old to plot; at any rate she dutifully did what the Queen wanted, and kept Arbella under strict super-vision. The situation dragged on until Arbella was in her late twenties and still unmarried; not unnaturally she grew to hate her grandmother, became increasingly involved in intrigue, and finally seems to have gone a little mad. Matters came to a head in 1603, a year of plots, rows and mounting tension at Hardwick, with Privy Councillors passing to and fro, Arbella in hysterics and Henry Cavendish involved in an intrigue to abduct her and possibly attempt to proclaim her queen. But it all came to nothing; Elizabeth died, declaring James I her heir on her deathbed; James took a fancy to Arbella, brought her to London and showered favours on her. She only returned to Hardwick for one short visit in 1605; in 1610 she made a surreptitious marriage to the Earl of Hertford, the most dangerous of possible claimants to the throne, and was sent to the Tower of London, where she died in 1615.

At Hardwick, after Arbella had left, peace returned to the ancient Countess for the remaining five years of her life. She died on 13 February 1608, with 'the blessing of sense and memory to the last'. Bess was buried in great state in the church of All Hallows, Derby, now the cathedral. The epitaph on her tomb celebrated her as the 'aedificatrix' of Chatsworth, Hardwick and Oldcotes.

(Right) Bess of Hardwick's magnificent tomb in Derby Cathedral

Chronicle of a death foretold

Legends later grew up of a prophecy foretelling that she would never die while she was building, and of the famously fierce winter of 1607–8 putting a stop to her building activities in spite of boiling ale instead of water being used to melt the mortar. Unfortunately, there is no evidence of any building activity in the last years of her life: Hardwick was finished, and so was her smaller house at Oldcotes, which she built for her son William and which has been demolished.

The building of Hardwick

'Higher yet in the very East frontier of this county, upon a rough and a craggie soile standeth Hardwic, which gave name to a family in which possessed the same: out of which descended Lady Elizabeth, Countess of Shrewsbury, who beganne to build there two goodly houses joining in a maner one to the other, which by reason of their lofty situation shew themselves, a farre off to be seene, and yeeld a very goodly prospect.'

William Camden's *Britannia*, 1610

(Above) To the right stands the Old Hall, which Bess rebuilt and retained after she decided to build the New Hall (behind the garden wall to the left). The Old Hall survives as a roofless ruin. A 17th-century drawing

Hardwick is fortunate in that the greater part of its building accounts has survived. They cover the period from 1587, when work on the Old Hall was already in course, until 1599, when work on the New Hall was approaching completion. In addition, two accounts books for the years 1591–8 and 1598–1601 have occasional references to building, besides, of course, giving fascinating information about life at Hardwick. An inventory of 1601 gives the original use of the rooms.

Hardwick Old Hall

For many visitors to Hardwick, it is a matter of amazement to find two such large houses existing side by side, especially when they learn that both houses were more or less fully furnished and in use at the same time; Hardwick Old Hall became ruinous only in the 18th century. When Bess started to remodel the Old Hall in about 1585, her husband was still alive, and she did not have the means to embark on anything as magnificent as the New Hall. As she and her husband were of an age, there was no especial likelihood that she would survive him.

The central portion of Hardwick Old Hall is irregular and gabled, perhaps representing in much-altered form the house that already existed when Bess took up residence. At either end she added two substantial and roughly balancing wings, with level balustraded parapets. At the top of each wing, above three storeys of comparatively low rooms, was a series of immense and lofty state rooms, lit by towering windows. One wing has a tower six storeys high, the other shallow projecting bays running all the way up. Possibly as a result of the haphazard way the house was built, it has the unique feature of two full-scale great chambers, the Hill Great Chamber and the Forest Great Chamber, at the west and east ends of the house. But perhaps the most revolutionary feature is the great hall, two storeys high, going across the centre of the house, in a position radically different from the conventional medieval one. Bess was to use this feature again to great effect.

Shrewsbury's death in 1590 improved Bess's financial situation and encouraged her to build the New Hall. But she continued to live in the Old Hall until the New Hall was ready for occupation in 1597; in fact the Old Hall was still

being finished while the new one was being built. Thereafter it was used to provide a useful supply of extra accommodation for both servants and guests. The size of the New Hall must always have been calculated with this in mind, for, large though it is, it was by no means large by comparison with other great Elizabethan houses such as Burghley, Holdenby or, for that matter, Chatsworth. On the other hand, the scale and splendour of the state apartment on the second floor suggests that it was specifically built in the hope of royal visits of a future Queen Arbella.

Both houses were built of the same stone, quarried just down the hill, and in many cases the same craftsmen worked on both of them, but the results were very different. The Old Hall looks as if it had been designed as it went

along; the New Hall is splendidly all of a piece. The difference reflects the more settled and prosperous conditions under which the New Hall was started, but also the fact that a new mind had got to work on its design. There is little doubt that its plan was provided by Robert Smythson (c.1535–1614), one of the most original of Elizabethan architects.

(Right) The Hill Great Chamber in Hardwick Old Hall. S. H. Grimm's reconstruction of 1785

Robert Smythson 'architect and surveyour'

The term architect is somewhat misleading, for the concept of an architect was only in its embryonic stages in Elizabethan England. Robert Smythson was trained as a stone-mason, almost certainly in London. By the 1560s he had become a master-mason, travelling round England with a gang of masons working under him. As such he was brought from London to Wiltshire in 1568 to assist in the rebuilding of Sir John Thynne's house at Longleat. He worked there on and off for eighteen years, carved much of the external detail himself and had a considerable influence on its design. In 1580 he moved on to Wollaton Hall in Nottinghamshire where he was surveyor rather than master-mason, both involved in designing the house and superintending its erection; by now he had stopped working as a mason. He settled at Wollaton and remained there until his death in 1614, when he was described on his monument in the church as 'architect and surveyour unto the most worthy house of Wollaton and divers others of great account'.

Among those 'divers others' was Worksop Manor in Nottinghamshire, which was remodelled to his design around 1585 for Bess's husband, the Earl of Shrewsbury. Bess may have had a hand in the first stages of its rebuilding,

but as it went up, her marriage finally exploded. Fear of upsetting a powerful patron may have made Smythson unwilling to work for Bess at Hardwick until after her husband's death.

The evidence that he provided designs for the new house at Hardwick is not absolutely conclusive, but it is extremely strong. The account book which may have contained payments for them has disappeared, but the general account book for 1597, the year in which the house was finished, records a gift on 27 March of £1 to 'Mr. Smythson the surveyour' and 10s to his son. Among the Smythson drawings, now belonging to the RIBA in London, is a plan unmistakably connected with Hardwick, though with minor variations. Robert and his son John subsequently did work for Bess's son Charles, including the design (by John) of Bolsover Castle, a few miles north of Hardwick. And stylistically Hardwick is a natural development from Longleat, Wollaton and, especially, Worksop.

Most Elizabethan houses were the result of teamwork, with patron and family, friends of the patron, an outside 'surveyor' and craftsmen on the spot all contributing; the idea of an 'architect' in command was only beginning to develop. Bess of Hardwick herself must have had strong ideas; her third son Charles was interested in architecture; the French painter John Balechouse, who was on and off acting as clerk of the works besides working as a decorator, certainly made important contributions. But the startling contrast between the disorganised grandeur of the Old Hall (pre-Smythson) and the integrated splendour of the New (post-Smythson), its architectural links with Longleat, Wollaton and Worksop, where Smythson had worked, all suggest his importance in giving form to Bess's aspirations.

On the other hand there is no evidence or likelihood that Smythson closely supervised the building of Hardwick. It was probably a case, as often happened with Elizabethan houses, of a 'surveyor' providing plans and elevations, leaving the detailing to the workmen on the spot, who made alterations to suit their own convenience or as dictated by the client while work was in progress.

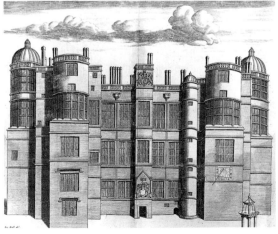

Worksop Manor as remodelled for the 6th Earl of Shrewbury by Robert Smythson, the architect of Hardwick

In Hardwick three of the most notable characteristics of the Elizabethans and their architecture reach culminating expression: their enthusiasm for symmetry and order; for what were called at the time 'devices'; and for huge expanses of glass.

Symmetry and devices

Symmetry applied to domestic (as opposed to ecclesiastical) architecture was essentially a Tudor innovation, and one can still sense at houses like Hardwick and Montacute the delight with which their builders balanced tower against tower and lined up the porter's lodge with the front door, between symmetrical pavilions. But at Hardwick not only the entrance front is symmetrical; the house is symmetrical on all four sides and its basic scheme of a rectangle surrounded by six towers, two to each long and one to each short side, is simple as an idea but ingeniously complex in its results, for the towers assume an endless variety of groupings according to the angle from which they are looked at. Examples of this type of ingenuity were called 'devices' by the Elizabethans. They used the term over a wide range to cover, for instance, buildings of complex or original plan, acrostic or riddle poems, and the jewels incorporating a symbolic picture and matching motto which courtiers devised to sum up their approach to life and wore when jousting in front of the Queen.

The unity provided by the four-way symmetry of the façades is further emphasised by the classical entablatures which run all the way round the house between each storey. The height of these storeys progressively increases, and their differences expressed the social importance of their function: basically servants and children on the ground floor, Bess herself on the first floor, potential royal

(Right) Queen Elizabeth's dress is decorated with flowers and mythical beasts that embody the Elizabethan love of 'devices'

visitors on the second floor. The importance of order and degree in society and all aspects of life, as a reflection of divine order in the universe, was ceaselessly hymned by the Elizabethans; Hardwick is a brilliant model of society, expressed in stone.

Various means were used to obtain complete all-round symmetry at Hardwick, and yet provide the rooms of all shapes and sizes that were needed. A few windows are completely false and have chimneypieces behind them. In a number of cases what seems to be one window on the exterior conceals two storeys; four low-ceilinged bedrooms, for instance, are concealed between the top lights of the left-hand windows on the entrance façade. More important, the Hall goes through the middle of the house instead of running along the entrance front; the latter was the normal arrangement, but was difficult to combine with a symmetrical façade.

'Hardwick Hall, more glass than wall'

This has become a familiar jingle. Other Elizabethan houses, including Smythson's Longleat, Wollaton and Worksop, had huge windows, but Hardwick went further than any of them. Nearly all the chimney flues are carried up through the internal walls leaving the external façades available for as much glass as could be provided with structural safety. These great windows were pursued by the Elizabethans and Jacobeans as status symbols (for glass was very expensive) regardless of comfort. Until the introduction of central heating, Hardwick, on its hill top, was bitterly cold in winter.

(Above)   The towering turrets of Hardwick

Building high

The impressiveness of Hardwick's glass façades is much increased by their height. High buildings seem to have appealed to Bess; Chatsworth, Worksop and Hardwick Old Hall were all unusually high buildings for their date. One reason for this was that they were a storey higher than was normal, for Bess liked to have her high-ceilinged state rooms up on the second floor, instead of on the first, as was usual at the time. And at Hardwick the house is made higher still by its six great turrets. The accounts show that these were altered in the course of building operations to increase their height, no doubt to obtain an even more impressive effect (few people, incidentally, notice that the north and south towers are higher than the others).

Other alterations were also made as the building went up. The loggias, for instance, were originally intended to run right round the building instead of only between the towers on the two main fronts; one can still see the line of rough stone at the corners where their roofs would have been tied in, but these portions were never built, probably because it was felt that they would make the rooms behind them too dark. The way in which both staircases gradually work their way to the turrets at either end of the house may also have been the result of a change of plan. The result is unique to Hardwick, and their long processional route through the middle of the house, especially that of the main staircase, with constantly changing views and contrasts of light and shade, is one of the most memorable features of the house.

Styles reconciled

Elizabethan houses such as Hardwick reflect a miscellany of stylistic influences; the result is often clumsy or indigestible, but not always so, and Hardwick is a memorable example of a mixture that works. The symmetry of its plan and layout, its two loggias, the classical entablatures that divide the storeys, and the crowning

> 'You shall have sometimes fair houses so full of glass, that one cannot tell where to become to be out of the sun or cold.'
>
> Francis Bacon

balustrades, show the influence of the Renaissance; its towers and huge grids of glass owe much to Perpendicular Gothic; its detail came from a number of sources, but much the strongest influence is the Mannerist architecture of the Low Countries, as popularised in England through the pattern books published at Antwerp by Vredeman de Vries and other architects. Among the most prominent features of this Flemish style was its use of obelisks and the motif known as 'strapwork' and these are omnipresent at Hardwick, modelled in stone, marble or plaster as overmantels throughout the two houses and crowning its silhouette on towers, lodges and courtyard walls.

Robert Smythson is unlikely to have had much to do with this detail, which was probably designed by the craftsmen working on the house, often working from engravings. Only the two magnificent chimneypieces in the Long Gallery relate to a Smythson drawing for a gatehouse and were probably designed by him. Anthony Wells-Cole and others have traced the sources of much of the plasterwork, carvings, panelling and embroideries at Hardwick New and Old Halls to Flemish engravings. The sources include Venus and Summer in the High Great Chamber; details in the hunting scenes in the frieze in the same room; Cybele in the Paved Room; the marriage of Tobias in the Blue Room; the figures of Judas and Mahomet in the embroideries of the Virtues; and other elements throughout the house. But at Hardwick, as in Elizabethan England as a whole, the craftsmen adapted, simplified and combined elements from different sources and added their own, with a zest and ingenuity that made the results intensely individual creations.

This engraving by van der Passe was the source for the image of Venus chastising Cupid in the High Great Chamber frieze

The craftmen of Hardwick

Many of the craftsmen at Hardwick had worked with each other before, either at Chatsworth or under Smythson at Wollaton. The greater part of the masonry was contracted for by John and Christopher Rodes, who had been the main contractors at Wollaton. Among other masons William Griffin carved the Hall screen and one of the stone surrounds on the Chapel landing (the latter jointly with James Adams). Two other masons, Henry Nayll and Richard Mallory, carved another of the Chapel landing doors and assisted Thomas Accres with the elaborate alabaster and blackstone decoration surrounding the door and chimneypiece in the Best Bedchamber. Accres, who had previously worked both at Chatsworth and Wollaton, was an important member of the Hardwick team, and the general payments to him in the accounts may cover chimneypieces in stone, alabaster or blackstone throughout the house; but payments for specific chimneypieces or plasterwork are regrettably absent from the accounts. The more elaborate plaster-work was probably modelled by Abraham Smith, who had been at Chatsworth; another, but otherwise unknown plasterer, John Marcer, made the ceiling of the turret banqueting house on the roof and did unspecified work in the High Great Chamber. Ballechouse, Accres and Smith remained full-time

'John Painter'

The Mannerist engravings that inspired the decoration of Hardwick may have been brought by one of the craftsmen working there, the painter John Ballechouse. He has recently been identified with Jehan Balechou, who was recorded in Tours in 1557. His French name was so indigestible to Derbyshire clerks that he is normally referred to in the accounts as John Painter. He first appears working for Bess at Chatsworth in 1578 and remained with her until her death, after which he was in charge of the mysterious building or decorating operations carried out at Hardwick by her son. In Bess's lifetime he was almost certainly responsible for the painted frieze in the Long Gallery, for the stencils of arabesques or strapwork which cover much of the panelling, and very probably for the painted cloths at present in the Chapel (illustrated).

(Above) The huge plasterwork frieze in the High Great Chamber was the work of Abraham Smith, who had previously been employed at Chatsworth

employees of Bess until her death, each being paid with a quarterly wage and lease of a farm.

From near and far

Stone, as already mentioned, came from the quarry down the hill, wood mostly from Bess's woods, and glass probably from her glassworks at Wingfield. Blackstone came from her quarries at Ashford in Derbyshire and was cut at a sawmill constructed by Thomas Accres in 1595 and referred to in the accounts as the 'engine'. Alabaster came from Creswell a few miles north of the house. Iron came from her ironworks at Wingfield, lead from lead workings at Winster, Aldwark and Bonsall, which Bess had handed over to her son William. So Hardwick was to a large extent a local product, built from local materials mostly drawn from Bess's own property and by local craftsmen or craftsmen who had been working for her over many years. In the same way many of the embroideries were worked either by Bess and her ladies or by professional embroiderers on her staff.

Tapestries and plate, on the other hand, had to be bought in London or elsewhere. The tapestries largely survive; the Aladdin's cave of sumptuous plate that covers page after page of the inventory has all vanished and was probably sold or melted down in the 17th century. No furniture appears in the Hardwick accounts, apart from a few tables and forms run up in the house by her own joiners. Probably much furniture was brought over from Chatsworth, along with embroideries, hangings, pictures and plate, as Bess lived here more and more.

Life at Hardwick

The upper servants

Hardwick, like other grand Elizabethan house-holds, was organised like a little court. At the centre was Bess herself and round her radiated three concentric circles: her own immediate family, the upper servants and the lower servants. The division between upper and lower servants was a crucial one in all big Elizabethan households. The upper servants were more like courtiers than servants in our sense of the word. They were usually the younger sons or daughters of good families, were known as 'Mr' or 'Mrs' and counted as gentlemen and gentle-women, as opposed to the lower servants, who were classed as yeomen. Bess herself had been in such service as a girl, and the gentlemen servants at Hardwick included (until he was sent away in disgrace in 1600) her own nephew, George Knyveton, the son of her half-sister Jane, who

(Left)
This scene from one of the needlework panels in the Hall evokes the courtly world of Bess's Hardwick (although it actually depicts the dissolute Sardanapalus feasting while his palace burns)

(Right)
Bess's female staff would have used embroidery frames like these.
A 16th-century woodcut

lived with her at Hardwick. The gentlemen were employed in running the estate as well as the household, for a separate estate office with its own staff was a much later development. At their head was the steward, normally the chief officer of the household and a person of great importance. But Hardwick was a woman-oriented household, and the best paid and probably most influential of the upper servants was Mrs Digby, the chief of Bess's gentlewomen; she was paid three times as much as her husband, who was also in the household. These gentlewomen were Bess's companions and assistants, entertained her guests and helped work the embroideries which are still such a feature of Hardwick.

The lower servants

The upper servants ran the stables and organised life in the upstairs rooms, but all the heavy work was done by the lower servants. The hall, kitchen, cellars and offices were run by the cream of the lower servants, the NCOs so to speak, of the household; at their head was the clerk of the kitchen, an important official whose responsibilities ranged far beyond the actual kitchen. Among his subordinates was the yeoman of the buttery, also known as the butler, who was in charge of the buttery and beer cellar and was a much less important figure in the household than the butlers of the 19th and 20th centuries. A distinctive feature of the work of

Always within call
The servants did not live apart in their own little world behind a green baize door, like the Victorian servants for whom an inconspicuous servants' wing was built at Hardwick in the mid-19th century. Self-contained servants' wings only became feasible through the invention of bell-pulls, connected by wires running from individual rooms to the long row of bells in the servants' corridor. Before that, servants had to be within calling distance.

the lower servants, as opposed to servants in big households two or three centuries later, was that it was the men who did most of the work. In addition to the waiters, the cooks and scullions were all men, and all the cleaning of the house was done by men. The only women among the lower servants were ladies' maids, nurses for the children (if there were any) and laundry maids, and the last worked outside the house.

Living together

As noble Elizabethan households went, that at Hardwick was not especially large. Bess had about 30 indoor servants of both ranks on her payroll. In addition Arbella had her own small staff, and the size of the household would have been increased by at least another ten when Bess's son William kept house with her, as he seems to have done for some of the year.
At Hardwick the servants slept all over the place. The upper servants had their own well-furnished rooms, mostly in the Old Hall. The lower servants bedded down more indiscriminately, on landings on the main staircase, outside Bess's bedchamber door, in the scullery, off the pantry and the hall, or in the porter's lodge and the turrets round the entrance court. In addition all the grander bedrooms had their 'pallets', a rolled-up straw mattress which could be pulled out at night for a servant to sleep on in the bedchamber or just outside the door, at hand to protect or serve his master or mistress.

A multi-purpose room
The Hall

During the daytime the lower servants ate, and when not otherwise employed sat, played cards and gossiped, in the Hall. The owners of great Elizabethan houses had long ceased eating in the hall, except on rare occasions. In some households their place at the high table was taken by the upper servants, presided over by the steward, but at Hardwick there was no high table in the hall, and only the lower servants ate there. There would probably have been 40 or 50 people in it at a busy period, for the outdoor servants ate there as well, as did visiting servants and Bess's little gang of resident craftsmen who were busy probably up to her death in finishing off the decorations of the house. These included Abraham Smith the plasterer and his son, Thomas Accres the mason and marble cutter, with his assistants Laurence Dolphin and Miles Padley, and John Ballechouse the painter with his son James. On feasts and holidays the room would almost certainly have been much more crowded; later account books show as many as 300 tenants, friends, servants and others being entertained at one go in and around Christmas and the New Year in the 1660s.

But this animated, companionable and noisy room was also the room through which all visitors, even the most important, had to thread their way, while the usher of the hall shouted 'silence my masters' in an effort to still the noise; all Elizabethan and Jacobean household regulations are full of instructions aimed at keeping down the noise in the hall. It seems strange to us that the servants' hall should also be the entrance hall. But most Elizabethan rooms served two or more purposes, even when, as at Hardwick, there was no shortage of space. Dining rooms were also sitting rooms, music rooms and ball rooms. Bedrooms were more like bedsitting rooms. Although Bess had her own withdrawing room, she conducted business and wrote her letters in the inner security of her bedchamber; here, as the inventory shows, she kept her writing-table and her books, and stored her papers and her money in a great iron chest and a miscellaneous series of coffers and boxes.

Rooms of state
The second floor

The fact that the functions of rooms were much less differentiated than they were, for instance, in Victorian times, does not mean that life at Hardwick was a haphazard affair. Bess must have lived in an atmosphere of continual ceremony. The arrival of an important guest was a ceremonial event and so was the serving of her food when she ate in state in the High Great Chamber, served by waiters on bended knee. Even the act of sitting down was a ceremony, for in each of the rooms she frequented she had her own special chair, decorated with gold or silver and with an upholstered footstool, necessary as well as ornamental because of the height of the chair. The house was divided not according to function, with living rooms below and bedrooms above, but according to state; on each floor the rooms grew more ceremonial.

The ceremonial pivot of the house was the High Great Chamber. In all large Elizabethan houses the great chamber had taken the place of pre-eminence held in the Middle Ages by the great hall. It was always the most sumptuously decorated room. Often, as at Hardwick, the decoration included the royal coat of arms as a demonstration of loyalty. It could be used for receiving and entertaining important guests, from the monarch downwards, or dancing and music, or for performing masques and plays: the Queen's players were at Hardwick in September 1600, and may have performed in the High Great Chamber or Long Gallery. But the principal use of a great chamber was as the room

> ### The role of the great chamber, according to a contemporary set of household regulations
> 'In that place there must be no delay, because it is the place of state, where the lord keepeth his presence, and the eyes of all the best sort of strangers be there lookers on … wherefore the gentleman ushers is to take a special care herein for their credit sake and honour of that place.'

(Above) The High Great Chamber

where dinner and supper were served with great ceremony whenever a great visitor was entertained or the lord or lady were 'keeping their state'. A key part of the ceremony was the actual arrival of the food, carried in a formal procession right the way up from the servery by the kitchen, through the great hall (where everyone present stood up in its honour) and up the interminable flights of the great staircase to its final destination in the great chamber.

Dinner was normally served at eleven in the morning, supper at five or six. At the end of each meal the family and guests retired to a withdrawing chamber next to the great chamber, while the remains of the meal were cleared away from the latter, and it was prepared for possible music or dancing later on. On the other side of the withdrawing chamber was almost always the best bedchamber, where important guests were installed. Great chamber, withdrawing chamber and best bedchamber form the standard ceremonial sequence in all big Elizabethan houses, and Hardwick was no exception. To this was usually added a long gallery, as at Hardwick. The long gallery was another multi-purpose room: it was used as an alternative reception room to the great chamber, for exercise in wet or cold weather, for the hanging of portraits, and above all, perhaps, as a status symbol.

For family and servants
The first and ground floors

Hardwick, like both the Old Hall and Chatsworth, had the unusual peculiarity of a second great chamber, known as the Low Great Chamber, on the first floor. This room (now the Dining Room) was probably the equivalent of a dining parlour, which was a normal feature on the ground floor of Elizabethan houses; the change of name may have been due to the fact that, because of Bess's idiosyncratic planning, the room is on the first floor, and parlours were always thought of as ground-floor rooms.

The Low Great Chamber, together with Bess's own withdrawing chamber linked to it by the gallery across the hall, and with her bedchamber and the chambers of William Cavendish and Arbella Stuart beyond it, made up a family and household suite, as opposed to the far loftier

The south turret (in the foreground) was used as a banqueting room

state suite with its similar sequence of High Great Chamber, Withdrawing Chamber and Best Bedchamber, on the floor above. The Low Great Chamber was used by Bess for eating in on less formal occasions and seems also to have been used as a common room by the upper servants; Arbella refers in March 1603 to a group of them gossiping in it and 'taking the advantage of the fire to warm them by'.

The low-ceilinged ground floor was occupied by the nurseries, and a few bedchambers, but mainly by the lower half of the hall and chapel, and by the kitchen and offices: the pastry, where bread was baked; the scullery; the pantry, where the plate, bread and table linen were kept, and which had access to the wine cellar; and the buttery, where beer was served and from which stairs led down to the beer cellars.

A meal with a view
The turrets

In 1601 the turrets on the roof were used only for storage, but the plasterwork overmantels and hooks for tapestry in the east and west turrets show that they were intended to be good bed-chambers. The south turret, with Bess's arms over the door, a moulded ceiling and no fireplace, was described in the building accounts as a banqueting room. The Elizabethan meaning of banquet was different from what it is today; it was a dessert course of sweetmeats, fruit and wine served either as a meal in itself or as a continuation of dinner or supper; like coffee today, it tended to be served in a different room. Banqueting rooms and banqueting houses were often built where there was a good view; at Longleat in the 1560s Robert Smythson had constructed a whole series of banqueting rooms in turrets up on the roof, as at Hardwick. In general, flat roofs in Tudor houses tended to be used for exercise in good weather and for the enjoyment of the view; it was while walking on the leads of his house at Chelsea that Sir Thomas More was assaulted by a lunatic who attempted to throw him over the parapet. At Hardwick there were originally four banqueting rooms, the one in the turret on the roof, a second on the ground floor at the southern end of the east

No mod cons

Sanitation was crude; the Old Hall had a tower full of privies built out over the hill-side, but this dates from after Bess's time; in the New Hall most bedrooms had chamber-pots and close-stools, the latter usually covered with leather. Bess had her personal close-stool in a little room off her bed-chamber; it was 'covered with blewe cloth sticht with white, with red and black silk fringe', but there were no backstairs and no amount of silk fringe can have offset the squalor of carrying the contents of the emptied close-stools down the two great staircases.

colonnade (now a bathroom with a mezzanine bedroom above it), a third in the garden house at the south-east corner of the garden, and a fourth in the north orchard, now the car-park.

Magnificence before comfort

Life at Hardwick would, by modern standards, have been magnificent rather than comfortable. The food must always have arrived tepid in the High Great Chamber at the end of its long cere-monial route from the kitchen, and the guests, though they wore more clothes than we do today, must frequently have been even colder than the food. The huge multi-windowed rooms were only warmed by open fires; at the end of her life Bess was feeling the weather, as is shown by the coverlets and 'counterpoynt of tapestrie' described as hanging before the windows and doors of her bedchamber in the 1601 inventory. Lighting was entirely by candles. Water was pumped up by means of a horse-operated wheel from a well to a conduit house to the south of the hall. This survives, and originally contained a lead cistern under its canopy. From there a lead conduit conducted the water to the New Hall, perhaps to the two 'sesterns of lead' in the Low Larder in 1601. It must have been carried through the house in containers, for there was no running water.

Hardwick after Bess

William, 1st Earl of Devonshire

Bess was succeeded at Hardwick by her second son William, who had been created Baron Cavendish of Hardwick in 1605. When his elder brother Henry died in 1616, he inherited Chatsworth, but Hardwick remained his principal place of residence. In 1618 (in consideration of a payment of £10,000 to the Crown) he was created Earl of Devonshire.

Between 1608 and 1612 he spent £1,163 5s 6d on Hardwick. The accounts were entered into a 'book of building' kept by John Ballechouse but unfortunately this has disappeared, and only the weekly totals survive, recorded in the general account book with no particulars. The sum is a considerable one in terms of Jacobean money values, and it remains mysterious what it was spent on. There is no individual building of any importance at

Bess's favourite son, William Cavendish (later 1st Earl of Devonshire), who inherited Hardwick

Hardwick which can be assigned to this time, but it is possible that the panelling in the High Great Chamber and the moulded ceilings in the Hall, Long Gallery, Mary, Queen of Scots Room and Banqueting Turret date from it. There was a second spurt of building in 1619–21, when a new wing was put up at the east end of the Old Hall, but this has since disappeared.

Extravagance and economy
The 2nd Earl and Countess

The Earl of Devonshire died in 1626. His son, the 2nd Earl, survived him by only two years and died in 1628, aged 38. He was as extravagant

The 2nd Earl and Countess of Devonshire

as his father had been careful and in his short life managed to make a sizeable hole in the Devonshire estates. He married Christian Bruce, daughter of Lord Bruce of Kinloss, who gained something of a reputation as a wise and witty lady, survived her husband for many years, and nursed the properties back to financial solvency. Their years as Earl and Countess produced two mementoes which were to have a curious and eventful history at Hardwick, in the form of two canopies which were set up in the High Great Chamber and Long Gallery. Canopies had originally been the prerogative of the royal family or of ambassadors, but in the 16th century were widely adopted by peers of the rank of earl and above and set up over a state couch or chair of state, on which they would sit to eat or receive visitors.

New fashions and old fittings

Hardwick was regularly used as an alternative residence to Chatsworth right through the 17th century, and was adapted to new fashions in house arrangement. Towards the end of the century, opposite and matching apartments, consisting of withdrawing chamber, bed-chamber and closet or cabinet on the formal French model then in mode, were formed to either side of the great hall on the first floor; one was probably for the Earl and the other for his wife. Closets or cabinets, highly finished little private rooms where favoured guests would be received for a tête-à-tête conversation, were a

new feature of upper-class life. Bess's with-drawing chamber and bedchamber were adapted for one suite with modish new joinery in the bedchamber; and the room through her bed-chamber, possibly the closet which used to accommodate her close-stool, was redecorated as a cabinet. The Low Great Chamber, Ship Bedchamber and Tobies Chamber were similarly adapted as a second apartment, with the Ship Bedchamber enlarged at the expense of the Low Great Chamber. On the top floor the Pearl (now Blue) Bedchamber was refitted in the same style.

These bedchambers and closets all have richly moulded doors, chimneypieces and overmantels of high quality; a similar door leading from the Low Great Chamber to the Ship Bedchamber was removed by the 6th Duke. Their redecoration may have been the result of visits by the Duke's architects William Talman and John Sturges; ten guineas was expended on the former in January 1687 'for Diet, Wine and Ale at Chatsworth and Hardwick being 7 weekes'.

The main purpose of Talman's visit to Derbyshire was to inaugurate the rebuilding of the south front at Chatsworth. In the next twenty years the 4th Earl (Duke of Devonshire from 1694) gradually remodelled or rebuilt the whole of Elizabethan Chatsworth. Odd fittings from the old house were sent over to Hardwick: wainscot came in 1690 and a chimneypiece in 1691. It is possible that the wainscot may have included the inlaid panels now framed on the Chapel staircase, and the coat of arms and window in the Mary, Queen of Scots Room; and that the chimneypiece may have been the 'Marriage of Tobias' chimneypiece now in the Blue Bedroom. Once Chatsworth was rebuilt, Hardwick must have seemed completely out of date by comparison. Until the end of the 18th century it was used less and less by the Caven-dishes. Semi-deserted by the family and in gentle decay, it began to acquire a reputation as a curiosity, an untouched survival from the past. This reputation was greatly boosted on completely spurious grounds: Hardwick became a place of pilgrimage as the house where Mary, Queen of Scots had been imprisoned.

The making of a legend

As early as 1708 Bishop Kennet stated in his *Memoirs of the Family of Cavendish* that Mary, Queen of Scots' 'chamber and rooms of state, with her arms and other ensigns, are still remaining at Hardwick; her bed was taken away for plunder in the civil wars ... ; some of her own royal work is still preserved.' Later generations of visitors thrilled with unjustifiable excitement as they walked through the rooms which had, in fact, been built, decorated and furnished well after her execution. By the mid-18th century Bishop Kennet had been improved on, and two beds reputed to have been slept in by Mary were on show. In 1760 Horace Walpole reported that 'the great apartment is exactly what it was when the Queen of Scots was kept there'. In 1762, according to the poet Gray, 'one would think Mary, Queen of Scots, was but just walk'd down into the Park with her Guard for half an hour. Her Gallery, her room of audience, her antichamber, with the very canopies, chair of state, footstool, Lit-de-repos, Oratory, carpets, and hangings, just as she left them, a little tatter'd indeed, but the more venerable; and all preserved with religious care, and papered up in winter.'
In 1794 Mrs Radcliffe, the author of the *Mysteries of Udolpho,* 'followed, not without emotion, the walk, which Mary had so often trodden, to the folding doors of the great hall' and described how on the top floor 'nearly all the apartments of it were allotted to Mary; some of them for state purposes; and the furniture is known by other proofs, than its appearance, to remain as she left it.'

(Right) This needlework panel bears emblems of Mary, Queen of Scots and may have been sewn by her while in captivity

The Mary, Queen of Scots Room as recorded by S. H. Grimm in 1785. The Queen's coat of arms appears over the door

One can see how all this came about. At Chatsworth the apartments where Mary actually had been imprisoned survived unaltered until their remodelling in the late 17th century. There was then nothing left at Chatsworth to connect it with Mary except for two buildings in the park. But interest in her, on the increase through the 18th century, naturally transferred itself to Hardwick, where there was a complete Elizabethan setting ready to receive it. No-one looked at the account books which would have shown up the whole story; and the top-floor rooms, complete with canopies, were ideal for adoption as her state rooms, as long as the embarrassing evidence of the coats of arms and a few dates were ignored. A touch of authenticity was added by the carved panel of her arms, probably brought over from Chatsworth, in the room that became known as her bedchamber.

The legend of Mary, Queen of Scots' imprisonment at Hardwick is indefensible, but it is worth pointing out that many of the Elizabethan furnishings and fittings at Hardwick today were originally at Chatsworth in Mary's time there. The famous embroidered hangings of heroines of antiquity, for instance, now framed in the Hall and on the Chapel landing, were shown to 18th-century visitors as the work of Mary; this they certainly were not, but they were equally certainly made for Chatsworth in and around 1575. Other embroideries at Hardwick carrying dates in the 1570s, and probably many of the undated ones, must originally have been at Chatsworth. So must many of the portraits, and much of the furniture; the inventory of Chatsworth made in 1601 shows that it was relatively unfurnished, and it must have been partially stripped to furnish Hardwick. More Elizabethan fittings came later, such as the overmantel in the Withdrawing Chamber, and, possibly, Mary's own coat of arms, the Marriage of Tobias chimneypiece in the Blue Room, and the intarsia panels on the Chapel staircase. So if Mary were to visit Hardwick today, she would find much that would be familiar to her.

The 18th century

'Never was I less charmed in my life. The house is not Gothic, but of that betweenity, that intervened when Gothic declined and Palladian was creeping in – rather, this is totally naked of either ... The gallery is sixty yards long, covered with bad tapestry and wretched pictures.'

Horace Walpole, 1760

The extent of the family's abandonment of Hardwick in the 18th century can be exaggerated. Notes made by the antiquary Richard Gough in 1760 show that the Cavendishes were still visiting and receiving there, and that the Duke of Cumberland had slept there in 1759. In the late 1780s the 5th Duke and his wife, the beautiful Georgiana, began to pay regular visits. In 1789 Lord Torrington recorded that 'much repair has been done within some last years', that the house was full of workmen, and that the dining room (the Low Great Chamber) was being repaired; he complained that all the new work was of deal 'and only befitting a farm-house'. It was around this period, probably about 1800, that the lower half of the chapel was closed off and converted into a steward's room. The fashionable country-house architect, John Carr of York, probably oversaw this and other work. According to his son, the 5th Duke used to dine in the Low Great Chamber 'as he supped at Brooks's, with his hat on, which his friends gave as the reason for his being so fond of Hardwick', while his wife spent there 'the happy part of a harassed life'.

'Like a great old castle of romance ... Such lofty magnificence! And built with stone, upon a hill! One of the proudest piles I ever beheld.'

John Byng, Lord Torrington, 1789

67

The Bachelor Duke

But it was his son, the 6th Duke, better known as the Bachelor Duke, who really left a mark on Hardwick; his influence there is almost as pervasive, though not as obvious, as that of Bess herself. He inherited from his father in 1811, at the age of 21, and died in 1858. Spoilt, lovable, lively, extravagant, and cut off from public life by his increasing deafness, he more than spent his immense income on building, buying and entertaining at his numerous houses. He largely rebuilt Lismore Castle in Ireland and Bolton Abbey in Yorkshire, and embellished and enormously enlarged Chatsworth. He described what he had done at Chatsworth and Hardwick in a delightful and discursive *Handbook* written for his sister Lady Granville and published in 1845.

At Hardwick attempts to live in the High Great Chamber and Long Gallery were abandoned. Of the former the Duke records that 'for one winter I dined with my friends in this room, which was more dignified than entertaining, and, in spite of all precautions, exceedingly cold'. Similarly he describes 'a vain attempt we made to pass some evenings in the Long Gallery; although surrounded by screens, and sheltered by red baize curtains, the cold frosty East wind got the better of us'. Instead he fitted up the Withdrawing Chamber as a library (the book-cases have since been removed) and used the Dining Room, and Bess's drawing room and bedroom on the first floor; it was in Bess's bedroom that he died in his sleep in 1858.

But his activities extended over the whole house. Hardwick was very empty when he inherited it but he filled it with additional furniture, portraits and tapestry brought from his other houses, from Chatsworth, Chiswick, Londesborough in Yorkshire, and Devonshire House in London. His approach was visual and romantic rather than scholarly or historical. The watercolours painted for him by David Cox and other artists give an idea of what he was after –

The Bachelor Duke, who loved Hardwick and did much to establish its present appearance by his restoration work and romantic refurnishing

an effect of great, but mellow richness, and romantic light and shade. He was prepared to use anything old, including work of the 16th, 17th and 18th centuries, to contribute to this effect, and his extensions and alterations at his other houses, and the sale of Londesborough in 1845, provided him with a constant supply of redundant furnishings. The feeling Hardwick tends to give today, of being a house where tapestry is used almost like wallpaper, dates from his time; it used to be even stronger, for a good deal of tapestry was removed at various times in the 20th century. He was the first person to hang tapestries on the main staircase: 'the dreary whitewash of these walls wanted decoration'.

'Though it appears old and unaltered, there
has been a great deal done in my time, to the
house that "Bess of Hardwick" built.'

The Bachelor Duke

With a fine eye for silhouette and disregard
for history he brought a late 17th-century state
bed, wrongly called Mary's, from Chatsworth
to the High Great Chamber and used the tester
and back of another Chatsworth state bed of
the same date to replace the canopy in the
Long Gallery. The High Great Chamber
canopy was restored for him by Crace, the
London decorator, then found too 'glaring' for
Hardwick, taken off to Chatsworth and replaced
by a made-up one. He employed Crace end-
lessly to restore, remount, and sometimes copy,
embroidery or materials, which were then
displayed framed, mounted on screens, or
upholstering neo-Elizabethan stools and chairs;
frames for the embroideries were made up out
of the yards of 17th-century egg-and-dart
moulding made available by the redecoration of
the Scots Apartment at Chatsworth. He blocked
up many windows in the Long Gallery 'making
the room warmer and giving more space and a
favourable light to the pictures'. He disinterred
the Elizabethan 'Apollo and the Muses' overmantel from a packing-case at Chatsworth and
set it up in the Withdrawing Chamber. He set
up Westmacott's statue of Mary, Queen of
Scots, originally intended for Queen Mary's
Bower at Chatsworth, in the Hall at Hardwick
(now on the east colonnade), though admitting
that 'she represents popular belief and tradition
in defiance of dates and facts'. What he did in
the way of minor alterations and moving round
doors and panelling will probably never be fully
worked out.

The Long Gallery in the Bachelor Duke's time; watercolour by David Cox

Lady Louisa's garden

The Bachelor Duke was succeeded as 7th Duke by his cousin, William Cavendish, Earl of Burlington. He had married Blanche, the daughter of the 6th Duke's favourite sister Lady Carlisle, but Blanche had died in 1840, and his daughter Lady Louisa Cavendish kept house for him. In 1865 she married Admiral Francis Egerton and left home, but in her later life her father and her brother, the 8th Duke, lent her Hardwick for the summer, until her death in 1907. As a young woman, she regrettably destroyed the state bed in the High Great Chamber, on the grounds that it was 'entirely devoured by moth'. But for many years she was a loving and careful custodian, and she left a worthy memorial, in the form of the garden.

In the 18th century there had been no garden at all at Hardwick. In the 1830s Lady Louisa's mother, Lady Burlington, was lent the house by the 6th Duke and laid out a garden in the entrance court; she planted the cedars, one of which is still there, and elaborate flower-beds, in the form of a huge ES, which were removed in the 20th century. Lady Louisa herself laid out the main garden on the south of the house in about 1870. It occupies the site of the original Elizabethan garden, but the plan of its cross-shaped walks, between yew and hornbeam hedges, was entirely due to her.

Evelyn, Duchess of Devonshire, whose husband inherited as 9th Duke in 1908, describes how Lady Louisa 'used to sit in the morning in the gallery making sketches and notes – the sun streaming on to her white hair and widow's cap – and she loved to talk about what she hoped we should do when we in our turn should have the care of the place. I think she left a benign and kindly atmosphere.'

Lady Louisa's formal garden in the late 19th century

Hardwick in the 1900s

As described by Lady Maud Baillie, the 9th Duke and Duchess's eldest daughter, who was born in 1896:

When we were children the house at Hardwick, large as it is, was kept quite beautifully during most of the year by only two housemaids, the 'odd' man and a daily lady (she was called a 'char' in those days), whose limited ambitions seemed to consist in a passion for scrubbing floors. As the whole ground floor is stone-flagged, the area involved was vast.

The housekeeper, an awe-inspiring little woman dressed in black silk, reigned supreme. She had a real love and a deep pride in the house. On one occasion, when asked if the house was haunted, she replied that once or twice Bess of Hardwick, who died some 350 years ago, had come to thank her for her care of the house, but, she added, 'Of course there are no ghosts'.

When the family went for their annual visit to Hardwick for shooting parties in the autumn, they were accompanied by an army of servants, every room was occupied, even some of the turrets, which were the footmen's bedrooms. The only access was across the roof, an alarming experience in the dark with a gale blowing. There was no gas or electricity, and the darkness of the rooms, lit only by a very small lamp or a candle, was terrifying.

By the time my family, consisting of my parents and seven children, first lived at Hardwick throughout the autumn and winter of 1908, four bathrooms had been installed. In Lady Louisa Egerton's day there were none. The hot water for the main bedroom and nursery floors had to be carried from one tap on the third floor landing. The portable baths used were of the 'hip' variety, or flat round ones, into which the hard worked maids poured a few inches of tepid water. Even with the addition of a nursery bathroom on the top floor, life was anything but luxurious. All the seven children lived up there with a nanny, under-nurse and nursery maid, also any visiting maids who might be staying at Hardwick with their 'ladies'. The older children had breakfast and tea on the refectory table in the Great Hall, supervised by the two governesses. (We had already had 40 minutes' lessons by then.) The 'school party' were promoted to the Dining Room for luncheon.

If there were many visitors, we were relegated to our own table in the bay window, which had always been known as 'The Monkey House'. The 'nursery party' had all their meals upstairs in the Day Nursery, i.e. three nurses, the latest baby and any other child under five; after that age one was promoted to the Dining Room. The transportation of nursery meals was a major operation. The tray containing the food for 'meat meals' was carried by the 'Odd Man'. All the other meals were carried by the nursery maid, who was probably only 14 or 15, but had to put up her hair when she left home to go 'into service' and also wear dresses to her ankles. As there were 97 steps in all it can be appreciated that her life was a hard one (though, as I remember them, they were generally smiling and frequently singing).

We must have been remarkably fit as children, as we climbed up and down these steps many times a day. We had to be down in the schoolroom at 7.15 for three-quarters of an hour's work before breakfast at 8.0. We did over 6 hours of lessons a day, but only 3½ on Saturdays, with a compulsory walk or ride morning or afternoon. Each activity meant a change of clothing, and the lacing up, or unlacing, of high laced boots. All clothing was under the supervision of the nanny, and was therefore kept on the nursery floor at the very top of the house. The idea of keeping coats downstairs or near the schoolroom was unheard of. There were two governesses, one French and one German, and not a word of English was allowed during meals. There was little co-operation between the two ladies, and, goaded by aggressive children, frequent Franco-Prussian wars took place.

During the Christmas holidays my brothers, sisters and any cousins who might be staying with us generally took part in a play. This was no voluntary or spontaneous effort which we enjoyed, quite the reverse. It entailed hours of work, both in learning our parts and in rehearsing. The first winter we spent at Hardwick, it was thought appropriate that we should act the Trial Scene from 'The Merchant of Venice', staged in the Long Gallery. It was a somewhat ambitious enterprise as the eldest actor (Portia) was only 14. I was the Duke, aged 12, and so deeply were the words drummed into me that I can quote the whole part now, at the age of 76.

Duchess Evelyn

Duchess Evelyn's care of Hardwick lasted from 1908 until the National Trust took over the house in 1959. In her husband's lifetime the family only went there for a few weeks every year, but after his death in 1938 it was left to her as a dower house, and she lived there continuously except during the war. For 50 years her strong character, lively curiosity and delicately incisive voice dominated the house. This period saw much careful restoration of the embroideries and tapestries at Hardwick. The Duchess repaired many of them herself, sitting with an assistant, often one of her daughters, in the window bay of the Low Great Chamber, where the light was best for restoration work. It was she who was responsible for reintroducing the rush matting (originally made locally) which is now such a feature of the house. After the Trust took over in 1959, she stayed as a tenant, but visited the house comparatively little in the short time before her death in 1960.

The National Trust

The National Trust has now owned Hardwick for almost half a century. In that time it has faced a daunting challenge in conserving the fabric and contents of a 400-year-old house. Hardwick was built at the limits of Elizabethan structural engineering, without the flying buttresses that support the glass-filled walls of medieval cathedrals. As a result, the walls of the rooftop turrets have started to spread. Until the 1980s, Hardwick was surrounded by coal-mines and coke works. The pollution they generated, driven by scouring rain, eroded the hall's stonework, which was also suffering from unsuccessful repairs made by the Society for the Protection of Ancient Buildings in the early 1900s.

So in 1965 the Trust decided to begin a new campaign of repairs, taking sandstone from the same quarry Bess had used. Like Bess, the National Trust has its own dedicated team of stone-masons at Hardwick, led by master-mason Trevor Hardy. A new exhibition in the disused Pump House building explains their work. The current repair programme, funded by the Heritage Lottery Fund, English Heritage and the Trust, was completed in 2005, but there is still much to be done to the outbuildings.

Before the Long Gallery windows were repaired, storm-driven rain used to spray up to a metre into the room, saturating the panelling and the lime plaster floor. Sunlight and air pollution have also damaged Hardwick's unique collection of tapestries and needlework, which the Trust is gradually conserving and redisplaying. The work of the conservator is never-ending, but Hardwick and its precious contents are now in better heart than for many years.

(Right) Duchess Evelyn pioneered the conservation of Hardwick's precious textiles. She is shown at work in the High Great Chamber in this painting by Edward Halliday